Too many of us, regardless of our familiarity with the stories of the Bible, are blind to the story of the Bible. We miss the forest for the trees. We fail to recognize how the Bible' to tell one mega-story. The macro-

Phil Vischer
Creator of Veggie Tales and

Jim Nicodem's purpose is to lay out, in straightforward, nontechnical language, many of the most important principles of interpretation. He does this so each person may know the foundational principles of biblical interpretation, and so understand many texts. In other words, Jim wants the church he serves, and many other churches, to be filled with men and women who will become better Bible readers.

D.A. Carson, PhD, Research Professor of New Testament at
Trinity Evangelical Divinity School,
Author of *New Testament Commentary Survey*

As a university professor on a Christian college campus, I can tell you that biblical illiteracy is on the rise. That's why the Bible Savvy series should be a prerequisite reading for everyone. Jim Nicodem puts the cookies on the bottom shelf by making the epic story of the biblical narrative understandable and accessible. The Bible Savvy series lays out the foundation and context for God's Word and then shows us in plain language how to apply the Bible's teachings to our lives step-by-step. It's phenomenal.

Les Parrott, PhD
Seattle Pacific University
Author of *You're Stronger Than You Think*

The compelling reality about the Bible is that it is full of fascinating details about God and His wise and redemptive oversight of the history of mankind. Unfortunately, the larger, more profound story often gets lost in the details. Like a master storyteller, Jim Nicodem takes us beyond the details and exposes the grand plot of Scripture. Jim's work in the Bible Savvy series will amaze many of us who have lived to master the details and will motivate all of us to stand in greater awe of the One who is navigating history to a good and glorious end.

Joseph M. Stowell
President, Cornerstone University

The Bible is one of the most precious possessions to a believer living in a restricted nation. I am constantly amazed by the hunger for biblical teaching expressed by those who face persecution daily. Their sacrificial passion should inspire us to rekindle our quest for biblical understanding. Jim Nicodem's Bible Savvy series is the kind of resource needed to reengage our hearts and minds with God's Word and renew a hunger for God's truth on par with our persecuted brother and sisters.

> James E. Dau
> President, The Voice of the Martyrs

Jim has done a masterful job in the Bible Savvy series! In these four concise books, Jim marches with clarity and skill into topics that would be difficult to tackle in a seminary classroom, much less in an American living room. And rather than a monologue, these books create a dialog among the author, the reader, their small group, and the living Word of God. These practical, approachable resources provide foundational training that is greatly needed by nearly every small group and leader I encounter.

> Greg Bowman
> Coauthor of *Coaching Life-Changing Small Group Leaders*
> Past executive director of the Willow Creek Association

Reading the four books in the Bible Savvy series is like getting a Bible college education in a box! The Lord is calling our nation to a Bible reading revolution, and these books are an invitation to be part of it.

> Hal Seed
> Author of *The Bible Questions* and *The God Questions*
> Lead Pastor, New Song Community Church, Oceanside, California

Living in the land of the Bible is considered a privilege by many, but the real privilege is to let the Bible become alive through us, in whatever land we may live. In the Bible Savvy series, Jim Nicodem not only helps us to understand God's plan to save us, but also His desire to change and shape us through His Word and Spirit in order to be a light in this dark world.

> Rev. Azar Ajaj
> Vice President and lecturer, Nazareth Evangelical Theological Seminary

To ignite a love for the God's Word in others is the goal of any spiritual leader. Communicating God's Word is the most important of all. Pastor Jim's Bible Savvy series is the tool, the guide, and the process for worship leaders to go into deep spiritual places. His biblical scholarship, communicated with such creativity, is exactly what is needed in worship ministry today.

> Stan Endicott
> Slingshot group coach/mentor
> Worship Leader, Mariners Church, Irvine, California

Jim Nicodem leads one of America's finest churches. Jim knows how to communicate the truth of the Bible that brings historical knowledge with incredible practical application. The Bible Savvy series is the best I have ever seen. Your life and faith will be enhanced as you use and apply this material to your life.

> Jim Burns, PhD
> President, HomeWord
> Author of *Creating an Intimate Marriage* and *Confident Parenting*

Pastor Nicodem is like a championship caliber coach: he loves to teach, and he stresses that success comes from mastering the basics. The Bible Savvy series will help you correctly interpret the best Playbook ever written: the Bible. Understanding and applying its fundamentals (with the help of the Bible Savvy series) will lead one to the Ultimate Victory . . . eternity with Jesus.

> James Brown
> Host of *The NFL Today* on the CBS television network

JAMES L. NICODEM

Bible Savvy

Hear from the author by
checking out the videos
on the Bible Savvy Series
with James Nicodem.

biblesavvy.com

MOODY
PUBLISHERS

Foundation
The Reliability of the Bible

James L. Nicodem

MOODY PUBLISHERS

CHICAGO

All Scripture quotations are taken from the *Holy Bible, New International Version*®, NIV®. Copyright ©1973, 1978, 1984 by Biblica, Inc.™ Used by permission of Zondervan. All rights reserved worldwide.

Published in association with the literary agency of Wolgemuth & Associates, Inc.

Edited by Jim Vincent
Interior design: Ragont Design
Cover design: Smartt Guys design
Cover image: iStockphoto

Library of Congress Cataloging-in-Publication Data

Nicodem, James L., 1956-
    Foundation : the reliability of the Bible / James L. Nicodem.
      pages cm. — (The Bible savvy series)
    Includes bibliographical references.
    ISBN 978-0-8024-0634-7
    1. Bible—Evidences, authority, etc. 2. Bible—Inspiration. 3. Bible—
Canon. I. Title.
BS480.N485 2013
220.1—dc23

                                                    2012044783

We hope you enjoy this book from Moody Publishers. Our goal is to provide high-quality, thought-provoking books and products that connect truth to your real needs and challenges. For more information on other books and products written and produced from a biblical perspective, go to www.moodypublishers.com or write to:

Moody Publishers
820 N. LaSalle Boulevard
Chicago, IL 60610

1 3 5 7 9 10 8 6 4 2

Printed in the United States of America

About the
Bible Savvy Series

I MET THE REAL ESTATE AGENT at my front door and invited him in. My wife and I were about to put our home on the market and I had called Jeff as a potential representative. As he sat down at our dining room table and opened his briefcase, I noticed a Bible perched on top of other papers. I asked Jeff if he was a Bible reader and he replied that he was just getting started. What had prompted his interest? He'd recently come across a list in *Success, Inc.* magazine of the most influential books recommended by business leaders. The Bible had been the most frequently mentioned book on the list. So, Jeff was going to give it a try.

My real estate agent isn't alone in his new interest in the Bible. According to a recent survey, 91 percent of those who have lately begun attending church were motivated to do so by a desire to understand what the Bible has to say to their lives.[1] That means nine of every ten visitors to church are intrigued by the Bible! But while they are curious about God's Word, they're also a bit intimidated by it. The Bible is such a daunting book, written in ancient times and addressed to vastly different cultures. Is it really possible to draw relevant insights from it for our lives today? People are returning to church to find out.

Ironically, while an interest in Bible knowledge can be detected among those who are new to church, it seems to be on the wane among many veteran churchgoers. When my oldest daughter enrolled at a Christian college, the president of the school addressed parents on opening day. He told us that the Bible comprehension exams of each incoming class of freshmen show less and less knowledge of God's Word. And then he added: "These kids are growing up in *your* churches." Evidently, many churches are not doing a good job of teaching committed believers how to read, interpret, and apply the Bible.

The Bible Savvy series has been written to help a wide spectrum of Bible readers—from newbies to seasoned Bible study leaders—get their arms around God's Word. This multibook series covers four essential Bible-related topics that Moody Publishers has made available in one set as a comprehensive manual for understanding God's Word and putting it into practice. *Epic* is the first of the four-book series.

An added bonus to the Bible Savvy series is the Study Guide. These questions, for personal reflection and group discussion, have been crafted by a team of small-groups experts. Together they form a comprehensive study guide. The guide is also available online at *biblesavvy.com* and may be downloaded and used for personal study or reproduced for members of a small group.

Four Things You Must Know to
Get the Most Out of God's Word

The four books of the Bible Savvy series will give you a grasp of the following topics, allowing God's Word to become a rich resource in your life:

1. *The storyline of the Bible.* The Bible is actually a compilation of sixty-six books that were written over a 1,500-year period. But amazingly there is one central storyline that holds everything together. You'll trace this storyline in *Epic* from Genesis to Revelation, learning how each of the sixty-six books contributes to the overall plot.

2. *The reliability of the Bible.* How did God communicate what He wanted to say through human authors? What are the evidences that the Bible is a supernatural book? How do we know that the *right* books made it into the Bible and that the *wrong* books were kept out of it? Isn't a text that was hand-copied for hundreds of years bound to be filled with errors? *Foundation* will give you answers to questions like

these—because you won't get much out of the Bible until you're certain that you can trust it.

3. *How to understand the Bible*. People read all sorts of crazy things into the Bible, and have used it to support a wide variety of strange (and sometimes reprehensible) positions and activities. In *Context* you will learn the basic ground rules for accurately interpreting Scripture. (Yes, there are rules.)

4. *How to apply the Bible*. It's one thing to read the Bible, and it's another thing entirely to walk away from your reading with an application for your life. Even members of Bible study groups occasionally do a poor job of this. Participants leave these gatherings without a clear sense of how they're going to put God's Word into practice. *Walk* will equip you to become a Bible doer.

Do You Have Savvy?

The dictionary defines *savvy* as *practical know-how*. It is my hope and prayer that the Bible Savvy series will lead you into an experiential knowledge of God's Word that will transform your life.

Many people have contributed to my own love and understanding of the Bible over the years—as well as to the writing of this book. I owe a huge debt of gratitude to them.

Mom and Dad made God's Word central to our family life, encouraging my siblings and me to memorize big chunks of it.

When I got to high school, I was a bit turned off to church, but I started attending a youth ministry in a neighboring suburb that was led by Bill Hybels. (These were pre–Willow Creek Community Church days, when dinosaurs roamed the earth.) Bill had (and still has) an incredible ability to open the Bible, read a passage out loud, and then drive home its application to the lives of his listeners. After a year of hearing him teach God's Word in such a life-impacting way, I went away to college and decided to major in biblical studies.

Two professors (among many) fanned the flame of my love for the Bible during my college and seminary years. Dr. Gerry Hawthorne taught me Greek New Testament at Wheaton College, and there are thousands of men and women in ministry around the world today who still remember his simple-but-powerful class devotions. He'd put one verse on the chalkboard (remember chalk?) and then tease out its significance for our lives—often with tears in his eyes. Dr. D. A. Carson taught me the Bible at Trinity Evangelical Divinity School. His books (and occasional phone and email exchanges) continue to shape me today. I aspire to have even a quarter of his passion for God's Word!

After school, as I started out in youth ministry, I began listening to cassette tapes (same era as chalk) by Dr. John

MacArthur. John is internationally famous for his verse-by-verse teaching of Scripture. Although he is occasionally more adamant about certain doctrines than I am (we agree on the essentials), his love for the Bible is infectious. John has set the bar high for all pastors who want to faithfully teach their churches God's Word. As my ministry continued, I found other communicators who whet my appetite for Scripture—many of them through their books, some of them currently through their podcasts. Thank you Lee Strobel, Joe Stowell, John Ortberg, Mark Driscoll, Francis Chan, Tim Keller, and many others.

Today, my desire to get people into the Bible is fueled by the five thousand-plus eager learners whom I have the privilege of pastoring at Christ Community Church of St. Charles, Illinois, and its regional campuses. I am especially grateful for both the staff and volunteer leaders who oversee almost four hundred Community Groups that are studying God's Word. And one of those leaders, who writes incredible Bible curricula and teaches scores of Bible-hungry women, is my wife, Sue. Her devotion to Scripture is a constant inspiration to me.

Lastly, a special thanks to my faithful assistant, Angee Jenkins, who helped to edit my manuscript, track down footnotes, and protect my writing time; and to my agent, Andrew Wolgemuth, who found a great publisher in Moody to make the Bible Savvy series available to you.

Contents

To watch Jim's introduction to Foundation,
scan this QR code with your smartphone or go to
www.biblesavvy.com/video/#foundation1.

Foreword

WHEN I HEAR A SERMON or read Christian literature, my mind is programmed to take it in the information in three different ways: as a Christ-follower, as a pastor, and as a Bible professor. As a Christ-follower, I am asking, "How will these truths help me to follow Christ more closely?" As a pastor, I want to know, "How will this communicator's style bring home the important truths of Scripture to others?" As a professor, I am curious, "Has the speaker or writer done his or her homework?"

As a follower of Christ, I could tell you how the truths you learn in the following pages will give you practical guidance and insight that will motivate you to jump into the Word of God and study it more fervently.

As a pastor, I could expand on the accessibility of Jim's illustration-rich style. (It's almost as if you have an hour-long appointment with Jim at Starbucks and you've just started the conversation: "Jim, you say that the Bible is God's playbook in this game of life. Tell me, in your own words, what are the most important things I need to know about this 'playbook'?")

But I won't go into those things. Instead, I want to speak as someone who has some expertise in biblical studies. Too many well-meaning Christian writers miss the mark, either by refusing to go beyond the most basic of concepts about the Bible or, in contrast, by expounding on the backgrounds of the Bible, yet relying on bad sources. The problem with the first scenario is that it leaves far too many adults with a seven-year-old level understanding of the most important book written. The problem with the second scenario is that we are left with outdated, slightly misleading, or sometimes just flat-out wrong information.

In case you think this isn't such a big problem, think again. When as an adult you visit the doctor, you want the seven-year-old-level explanation for what ails you. You *do* want to hear your illness understood against the background of the latest medical research, all explained in layman's terms. Call it simplicity on the other side of well-researched complexity.

The beauty of this book is that it represents simplicity on the further side of the complex. If you have intellectual questions about the authority of the Bible and don't know where to begin, begin here. You won't be sorry. Jim Nicodem has done his homework.

> NICHOLAS PERRIN
> Professor of biblical studies, Wheaton College
> Author of *Lost in Transmission: What We Can Know about the Words of Jesus*

Introduction:
A Rock-Solid Foundation

IN THE FALL OF 1970, Marshall University's football team had just lost a closely fought game to East Carolina University, 17–14. The players climbed aboard their chartered plane for the flight back to West Virginia, where family and friends waited. But they never made it home. The plane crashed and everyone on board was killed: thirty-seven football players, the coaches, team physician, booster club parents . . . everyone.

The campus community of Marshall University grieved deeply. And then they began to rebuild their football team from scratch. They had a hard time recruiting a head coach, because nobody wanted the job of leading a team that would be made up almost entirely of freshmen. But they eventually found a guy who was crazy enough to take the job. And he recruited high school seniors from around the country. The NCAA helped by giving the Thundering Herd special permission to let freshmen play on the varsity squad.[1]

So Marshall University had a coach and they had players, but they lacked one essential ingredient for building a football team: a playbook. You see, the old playbook wouldn't do. They needed a playbook that could transform a group of inexperienced freshmen into a varsity team. They needed a playbook that would be basic and uncomplicated, but effective. Somebody mentioned that a neighboring school, West Virginia University, had a basic and uncomplicated playbook. Maybe they would share it with Marshall?

Yeah, right! How many coaches would be willing to loan their playbook to another team? Well, in this particular case, West Virginia University had a generous coach who was willing to do just that. His name was Bobby Bowden and he later became famous as the "winningest coach in college football." (Bobby has also shown me great generosity by writing the foreword to my first book, *Prayer Coach*. I love that guy!) Bobby Bowden's playbook was foundational for rebuilding Marshall University's football team. It was foundational for transforming a group of raw recruits into real players.

God has a playbook. And God's playbook is foundational for transforming us into real players on His team. God's playbook is called the *Bible*. That title comes from a Greek word that means, simply, book. The Bible is God's book, and God wants us to build our lives upon it. The writer of the old hymn "How Firm a Foundation" captured this truth in the opening line of his song: "How firm a foundation, ye saints of the Lord, is laid for your faith in His excellent Word!"[2]

Back in Old Testament days, Moses reminded God's people that they were especially privileged to be the recipients of God's written Word: "What other nation is so great as to have their gods near them the way the Lord our God is near us . . . ? And what other nation is so great as to have such righteous decrees and laws as this body of laws I am setting before you today?" (Deuteronomy 4:7–8). For us, too, it's a tremendous blessing to have a book from God that can shape and direct our lives. It's a special privilege to be the people of God's book.

Of course, all this assumes that the Bible *is* God's book, that it has truly come from Him. That its claim to be His Word to us is credible. That it is free of errors that would mar its trustworthiness. Only when we are certain that the Bible is a rock-solid foundation will we be motivated to build our lives upon it.

In *Foundation* you will learn how God authored the Bible (chapter 1); protected the Bible from errors over centuries of transmission (chapter 2); reveals Himself and His will to you through the Bible (chapter 3); and expects you to saturate your life with the Bible (chapter 4).

{ 1 }

God's Autobiography

CITY RESIDENTS FOUND LITTLE comfort as they sweltered under the summer sun on August 1, 1885. But relief was on the way. Six and one-half inches of torrential rain fell on Chicago over the next twenty-four hours.

Unfortunately, this produced major flooding. Sewage from the city's 750,000 residents and runoff from the infamous stockyards washed into the Chicago River. The polluted water was then carried out into Lake Michigan. According to an exaggerated story in the *Chicago Tribune* at the time, this toxic brew was then sucked up by the intake system that provided the city with its drinking water.[1]

The *Tribune*'s story was very alarming—even if it was suspect. Chicagoans started talking about the possible outbreak of cholera, dysentery, typhoid, and other waterborne diseases. Somebody suggested, although nobody remembers *who* said it, that people were dying from these diseases.

It was eventually claimed that one out of eight Chicagoans had succumbed to the epidemic. This part of the story was repeated again and again over the following years, without any supporting evidence. Each successive retelling merely parroted the previous accounts.[2] Today those events are known as the Chicago epidemic of 1885.

In 1956, Chicago's water sanitation department actually distributed an official pamphlet describing the 1885 epidemic. It was politically motivated; the sanitation department wanted public support for projects that would upgrade Chicago's water purification system.[3] But sanitation officials knew the voters were aware of the many improvements that had already been made in this regard (such as filtration and chlorination systems), which now ensured safe drinking water. So in order to get their money, they decided to put a little scare into the local population. They printed a pamphlet that retold the story of the 1885 epidemic.

Fast-forward to recent times. In 2000 Libby Hill wrote *The Chicago River*, a history of the river's impact on the city and surrounding environs. The Northern Illinois University professor included a section on the 1885 epidemic. In her research for the book, she couldn't find any evidence for the story of a massive epidemic. In fact, Hill discovered that the death rate for 1885 was actually *lower* than for previous years. That got her thinking: If one out of eight people had died, as the epidemic story claimed, there would've been dead bodies everywhere (almost 94,000 of them)! But there weren't. And the city would've come to a grinding halt. But it hadn't.[4]

Well, it turns out that the Chicago epidemic of 1885 was a tall tale. Even the environmentalist group Friends of the Chicago River was forced to take the story off its website.[5]

Could this account serve as a metaphor for how the Bible came into existence? Is the Bible nothing more than a collection of tall tales? Have the Bible's stories been exaggerated from the beginning? Have they been stretched so that the storytellers could advance their own agenda? Has contemporary research now proven these stories to be fabrications?

Bottom line: Is the Bible reliable?

In this chapter, I will begin to answer this question (in the affirmative, of course) by making the case that the Bible has come to us from a trustworthy God. This book is, amazingly, *God's Autobiography*. And that means that it is marked by three unique, reliability-affirming characteristics—it is supernatural, inerrant, and authoritative.

A Supernatural Book

A key text for understanding the Bible's authorship is 2 Timothy 3:16. This is a verse worth memorizing. For now, I just want to roll out its opening phrase: "All Scripture is God-breathed . . ." What does the expression *God-breathed* mean? In the old King James Version of the Bible, the word *inspired* was used instead of *God-breathed*. Why didn't the translators of our contemporary New International Version stick with *inspired*?

The NIV translators most likely dropped the word *inspired* because it wouldn't communicate to a contemporary audience what the apostle Paul meant to say when he wrote 2 Timothy 3:16. When we use the word *inspired*, we're usually referring to a person who's been emotionally or creatively moved to do something. I might say, for example: "I was inspired to clean the garage this past week." (Believe me, it would take inspiration!)

Or to use a classier example, we might say that George Frideric Handel was inspired when he composed his famous oratorio, *Messiah*. Here's a guy who wrote 260 pages of music for a complete orchestra in just twenty-four days. He didn't leave his room the entire time. He barely touched his food.[6] And when *Messiah* was first performed in 1742, it was so majestic that the King of England rose to his feet when the choir began to sing the *Hallelujah Chorus*. Yes, Handel was inspired. He was creatively moved.

But that's *not* what the apostle Paul meant to say about Scripture in 2 Timothy 3:16. The best English translation of Paul's original Greek expression is, in fact, exactly what we have in the NIV: "All Scripture is God-breathed." So, when theologians today use the old KJV word *inspired* to refer to the Bible, this is what they're talking about: the God-breathed nature of the book.

But what exactly is it about the Bible that is inspired or God-breathed? There are two mistaken notions with regard to inspiration. Some people assume that this must be a reference to the Bible's *writers*. Men like Moses and King David and the apostle Paul, who penned various books of the Bible, were inspired, right? Didn't God breathe into them some general ideas, after which they sat down and wrote out, as best they could, their particular portions of the Bible? No, that would be the first wrong notion.

The trouble with this view of inspiration is that it leaves open the possibility that these human writers might not have gotten things right. What if they misunderstood what God breathed into them to say? Or what if they didn't choose the best words to communicate these general God-given impressions to us? No, it's not enough that the *writers* themselves were inspired.

A second mistaken notion is to assume that inspiration refers to the Bible's *readers*. When you pick up the Bible and read it, God speaks to you. You, as it were, become inspired. Make sense? Some people who hold this view have gone so far as to say: "The Bible is the Word of God when it becomes the Word of God to you." Huh? What if that doesn't happen? What if you read the Bible and it doesn't feel like God is speaking to you? Is the Bible only inspired when it connects with you? Is it only inspired when you, as the *reader*, are inspired?

No. Inspiration is not about the Bible's *writers* and it's not about the Bible's *readers*. It's about the Bible's *words*. Go back to the opening phrase of 2 Timothy 3:16: "All Scripture is God-breathed." What is "God-breathed"? (Sorry to ask the obvious.) *Scripture is*. The Greek word for Scripture is *graphe*, and it means, literally, *writing*. So the writing itself, the very words that appear in print, is what God inspired. That's why theologians, when they speak of inspiration today, will often add the adjective *verbal* in front of it. "*Verbal* inspiration" clarifies the fact that God breathed out the actual words of the Bible.

WHAT GOD wanted to say got said, exactly as God wanted it said.

Why is this so important to note? Because it assures us that what God wanted to say got said, exactly as God wanted it said. Does this mean that the human writers (Moses, David, Paul, and so on) were simply secretaries, stenographers to whom God dictated His Word? Absolutely not. If you read the Bible, which is a compilation of sixty-six books, you'll quickly discover that each book reflects the vocabulary, the culture, the historical setting, and the personality of its human author.

For instance, compare Moses' laws with David's psalms, or with Paul's letters, or with Solomon's proverbs, or with Zechariah's prophecy, or with Matthew's biography of Jesus, or with Luke's history of the early church. There's a lot of variety among the books by those seven writers. That variety reflects the differences among the human authors. God didn't dictate His Word to them in some uniform fashion. However, God *did* ensure that what He wanted to say got said, exactly as He wanted it said. "All Scripture"—the writing itself, the very words that appear in print—"is God-breathed."

That makes the Bible a unique book. It's unlike any other book you can pick up at Barnes & Noble, or Amazon.com, or the public library. The Bible is *God's* Word. And because it is the Word of a supernatural God, it must be a supernatural book.

I know that sounds like an outrageous claim, especially if you are a skeptic as you read this. You probably think that I'm pretty gullible to believe that the Bible is God-breathed just because 2 Timothy 3:16 says that it's God-breathed. Well, I assure you that I have just as much of an aversion to being caught gullible as you do. I am very wary about being taken for a ride down fantasy lane.

I remember, years ago when I was a college student, taking a walk on a starry night with this good-looking girl. She began to point out constellations to me in the brightly lit sky. The Big Dipper was easy to spot. So was Orion's Belt. But as we continued to stroll, she began identifying starry configurations that I had never heard of. And when she'd ask me, "Do you see such-and-such?" I would nod my head and say uh-huh, even though I couldn't quite make out the cluster of stars that

BECAUSE IT is the Word of a supernatural God, the Bible must be a supernatural book.

she was describing. Constellation after constellation, my astronomy lesson continued. Wherever my date pointed, I would gaze and say: "Wow! That's cool!!"

About twenty minutes into the walk, an awful thought popped into my head: *What if she's making all this up?* What if she's playing a practical joke on me to see how gullible I am? What if I've been nodding my head and oohing and aahing over constellations that don't exist? What if she goes back to her dorm and tells her roommate: "You wouldn't believe the loser I suckered tonight!"

Nobody likes to be thought of as gullible . . . naïve . . . clueless . . . simpleminded. And that's why, in today's culture, it's a bit intimidating to express a belief in the Bible as God's Word; to claim that it's a *supernatural* book. No Western-civilized, college-educated, self-respecting man or woman believes that *God* authored the Bible. C'mon! Why should anybody swallow the 2 Timothy 3:16 statement that the Bible is God-breathed?

Evidence for a Supernatural Book

Very briefly, let me give you some hard evidence that points to the *supernatural* nature of the Bible. None of these proofs is conclusive in itself. But when you take them all together, they make a pretty strong case that this book has been authored by God.

Historical accuracy. When it comes to its many references to people, places, and events, the Bible is an amazingly accurate book. So say archaeologists. I'll talk more about this in the next chapter when I cover how it was determined which books to include in the Bible, because historical accuracy was a critical test that had to be passed. But let me note Luke's Gospel and the book of Acts as a quick example of the Bible getting its facts straight. Christian author and apologist Lee Strobel cites a highly esteemed archaeologist in his book *The Case for Christ*, who examined every one of Luke's references to thirty-two countries, fifty-four cities, and nine islands. And he didn't find a single mistake![7]

Fulfilled prophecy. Did you know that prophecy is fairly rare in the writings of most religions? In all the works of Buddha and Confucius there is not a single example of predictive prophecy. In the entire Quran, written by Muhammad, there's only *one* prophecy—and it's pretty general.

By way of contrast, the Bible's Old Testament alone contains over two thousand predictive prophecies. These are not vague predictions, like the kind you'd find in a fortune cookie. Many of them are very specific.

Consider just a few of the prophecies made about Jesus Christ, hundreds of years before His birth. (I refer to these prophecies, as well, in chapter 3 of *Epic* and show how they contribute to the Bible's overall storyline.) Daniel foretold the exact time of Jesus' appearing (Daniel 9:24). Micah predicted that Jesus would be born in the small village of Bethlehem (Micah 5:2). Zechariah prophesied that Jesus would enter Jerusalem triumphantly on the back of a colt, but later be betrayed for thirty pieces of silver (Zechariah 9:9; 11:12–13). Isaiah described how Jesus would be put to death alongside criminals, and yet be buried in a rich man's tomb (Isaiah 53:9). Prophecies like these surely evidence the Bible's supernatural character.

Indomitable durability. Time and again throughout history, the enemies of Christianity have attempted to undermine or even stamp out the Bible. But such efforts, though sustained, have all proven unsuccessful. My favorite anecdote in this regard concerns eighteenth-century French philosopher and skeptic Voltaire. Voltaire was a caustic critic of the Bible. He described it as a book of fairy tales that would cease to exist within a generation or two of his lifetime. It turns out that Mr. Voltaire wasn't much of a prophet. After his death, his house was purchased by a printing business that published copies of—would you believe—the Bible! Got to love God's sense of humor.

Overall consistency. Keep in mind that the Bible is actually sixty-six books in one. And yet its authors—who represent a wide variety of vocations, come from three different continents, and write over a period of fifteen hundred years—speak with remarkable harmony about *one* central theme. Imagine such a diverse collection of writers today agreeing on any topic, whether it be medicine or economics or sports or you name it.

A REASONABLE case can be made for the Bible being God-breathed based on its historical accuracy, fulfilled prophecy . . . and transformed lives.

Miraculous depictions. If the Bible is God-breathed, if it's a supernatural book, wouldn't we expect it to contain stories of God's miraculous interventions in our world? And yet, ironically, this is the very thing that skeptics won't tolerate about the Bible. Thomas Jefferson is a case in point. Are you familiar with Jefferson's New Testament? Jefferson was a true child of the Enlightenment, with its emphasis on scientific investigation. If something couldn't be studied or tested in the laboratory, ol' Tom wouldn't believe it. So one day he got out his X-ACTO knife and cut out all the passages in the Gospels that describe Jesus' miracles.

Let me tell you what's so wrongheaded about Jefferson's approach. Historical events are not proven by testing them in a science lab. We verify historical events by checking out the eyewitness accounts of those events. That's how we know that George Washington crossed the Delaware River in December of 1776, and that Abraham Lincoln delivered the Gettysburg Address in November 1863, and that the Chicago Cubs won the World Series in October 1908 (as unbelievable as that last event seems). Eyewitnesses attest to each of these events. And that's how we know that Jesus did miracles: eyewitness accounts.

Transformed lives. I've been the pastor of Christ Community Church for almost thirty years. During the past three decades, I have collected several files' worth of letters from people who claim that the Bible teaching they've received from my sermons and in our community groups has changed their lives in dramatic ways. Broken marriages have been reconciled, destructive addictions have been conquered, life-purpose has been discovered, character has been reformed, difficult trials have been endured, and concern for others has been developed. And people give the credit for these positive transformations to the impact of the Bible in their lives!

Is the Bible God-breathed, as it claims to be in 2 Timothy 3:16? Is it a supernatural book? A reasonable case can be made for this position based upon the Bible's historical accuracy, fulfilled prophecy, indomitable durability, overall consistency, miraculous depictions, and transformed lives.

An Inerrant Book

What does *inerrant* mean? It means that the Bible is free from any kind of error. In the preface of a book, an author often will acknowledge all the people who helped shape that book: the mentors, the colleagues, the researchers, the editors. And then the author will make a disclaimer that goes something like this: "While I wish to thank all these people for contributing to my book, any errors that you find in these pages are entirely mine." That's a nice, generous, humble thing to say. But you won't find God saying that about His book. Why not? Because it's inerrant!

Why should you believe that the Bible is inerrant? On the basis of three testimonies. First, there is *the testimony of God's character*. The Bible repeatedly refers to God as "the God of truth" (Psalm 31:5; Isaiah 65:16). The apostle Paul tells Christ followers that God has promised us eternal life, and then Paul adds: "God . . . does not lie" (Titus 1:2). The writer of Hebrews makes this same claim even more starkly: "It is impossible for God to lie" (Hebrews 6:18). God is truthful through and through. So, when God speaks, it is reasonable to conclude that His words are true. They're inerrant. Free from any kind of error.

Psalm 119 is the longest chapter in the Bible: 176 verses. And this psalm is all about God's Word. One of the things that it repeatedly affirms about God's Word is that it's true: "Your law is true . . . All your commands are true . . . All your words are true . . ." (Psalm 119:142, 151, 160). You get the idea. Because God is the *God of truth*, because God's character is 100 percent true, God's Word, the Bible, must be true.

Here's a second reason to believe that the Bible is inerrant: *the testimony of Jesus Christ*. Jesus obviously believed that Scripture is trustworthy and true. He affirmed this in one of His prayers: "Father . . . your word is truth" (John 17:1, 17). And He constantly **JESUS BELIEVED that Scripture is trustworthy and true, and affirmed this in one of His prayers.** quoted the Old Testament to back up His teaching, beginning these citations with the words "It is written." In other words, Jesus cited Old Testament stories as if He took them at face value. Stories about Noah and the flood, the destruction of Sodom and Gomorrah, God's miraculous provision of manna in the wilderness, Jonah spending three days in the belly of a giant fish—Jesus seemed to accept all these accounts as being historically accurate.

And Jesus didn't merely believe that the Bible is true in a broad brushstroke sort of way. His position was *not*: Scripture is true, generally speaking, even if some of the details are in error. No! Jesus said that not even "the smallest letter [or] the least stroke of a pen" in God's Word would disappear until it had all been fulfilled (Matthew 5:18).

A third reason to believe the Bible's inerrancy is *the testimony of logic*. This would be a good time to acknowledge that there are some Christian Bible scholars who don't care for the word *inerrant*. There are some who want us to believe that the Bible is basically trustworthy, even though it's not without error. "But that's OK," these scholars say, "because God is still able to get His message across, in spite of the errors that are sprinkled throughout Scripture." I struggle with the illogic of that perspective.

Does it make sense to you that God would speak His *truth* through statements that are occasionally *false*? (And if you point out that God speaks His truth through faulty pastors every Sunday, I would ask you how you know that these pastors are occasionally faulty. Isn't it by comparing what they say with God's faultless Word?) Furthermore, if some of what we read in the Bible is in error, who decides which statements those are? It seems to me that this position would allow us to reject portions of the Bible we don't like with a dismissive, "Oh, that's one of those errors."

I believe that the Bible is inerrant because the God of truth breathed it out, because Jesus accepted it as totally trustworthy, and because it makes logical sense that God would not leave us guessing about which parts are true and which are not. However, this doesn't mean that there aren't places in the Bible that *appear to be* in error. Let me give you several reasons why people sometimes mistakenly assume that they have found errors in the Bible.

Figures of speech are taken literally. For example, the Bible talks about "the four corners of the earth" (Revelation 7:1). Does that mean that the Bible contains scientific errors? After all, this is a description of a flat earth, right? Hardly. It's a poetic figure of speech that's not intended to be taken literally. Same thing when the Bible speaks of the sun *rising*. We all know that the sun doesn't rise. But that doesn't make the Bible wrong any more than it makes the TV weatherman wrong when he tells us the time of tomorrow's sunrise.

Narratives are not always arranged chronologically. Sometimes when the Bible tells a story, it relates the events of that story in the order in which they occurred. But other times the Bible relates the events thematically or topically (e.g., lumping together several

PEOPLE SOMETIMES assume that they have found errors in the Bible when they take figures of speech literally.

of Jesus' miracles or parables). So if one of the Gospels tells us that Jesus did things in a certain sequence, and another Gospel tells us that He did those things in a different sequence, that doesn't mean that one of the accounts is wrong. It means that one of the accounts has not been arranged in chronological order.[8]

Imprecise quotations are used. What if Matthew records that Jesus said something one way, and Mark's quote of Jesus is a little bit different. Is somebody in error? Nope. We do this all the time, don't we? We say: "My boss said . . ." or "My wife said . . ." or "My doctor said . . ." And then we give a summary, not an exact quotation, of what they said. In fact, the very next time we summarize what they said, we will probably do it a little bit differently.

Numbers are rounded off. Let me ask you a question. How old are you? On the count of three, I want you to call out your age. One . . . two . . . three! (Pause for your participation.) I bet you called out your age in a round number. I bet you said: "fifteen" or "thirty-three" or "fifty-seven." Am I right? But that's how old you were on your last birthday. That's not how old you are today. Your current age, to be precise, is a matter of years and months and days. Sometimes in the Bible, we read two different accounts of the same event, and the numbers are not exactly the same. An error? No, just rounded-off numbers.

I could add to this list of mistaken assumptions about errors in the Bible, but I think you get my point. Many of these so-called errors can be quickly straightened out with fairly simple explanations. (If there is a particular discrepancy about which you'd like some clarification, you'll probably find it covered in Norm Geisler's *When Critics Ask: A Popular Handbook on Bible Difficulties* [Baker].) Yes, I will admit that there *are* some discrepancies in Scripture that are still difficult, even impossible, to fully explain. But considering the Bible's overall track record for inerrancy, I'm prepared to give God's Word the benefit of the doubt in these cases.

An Authoritative Book

A couple of years ago, Sue and I met with our financial consultant and he suggested that we consider refinancing our mortgage. He gave us several good reasons for doing this: the low interest rates, the short amount of time it would take to recover the cost of the refinancing, and so on. In brief, our financial consultant said, "Go for it!" So we . . . didn't.

It's not that we don't trust our financial consultant. He gives great advice. But in this particular case, considering that our mortgage was almost paid off and a few other factors, we decided to sit tight. We're allowed to do that. We're not expected or required to obey everything our financial consultant says to us. He may be an expert, but he's not our final authority.

Many people respond to God's Word in a similar fashion. They treat it as if it's full of good suggestions. Kind of like the suggestions one might get from a teacher or coach or counselor or friend or investment analyst or Oprah. Please don't make the extremely dangerous mistake of dismissing God's Word as so many suggestions. God's Word is not advice—it is to be the final authority in our lives. Take a look at a story that Jesus told to illustrate this point:

> "Therefore everyone who hears these words of mine and puts them into practice is like a wise man who built his house on the rock. The rain came down, the streams rose, and the winds blew and beat against that house; yet it did not fall, because it had its foundation on the rock. But everyone who hears these words of mine and does not put them into practice is like a foolish man who built his house on sand. The rain came down, the streams rose, and the winds blew and beat against that house, and it fell with a great crash."
>
> When Jesus had finished saying these things, the crowds were amazed at his teaching, because he taught as one who had authority, and not as their teachers of the law. (Matthew 7:24–29)

Please note that both of the builders in the story represent people who have heard Jesus' teaching. They are like people who go to church and listen to sermons. The difference between the two groups is that the wise builders *do* what Jesus says to do (houses on rock) and the foolish builders *don't* (houses on sand). Are you responding to the Bible these days as if God Himself were looking you in the eye and giving you directives? Because He is. The Bible is *God's* Word. That makes it authoritative.

If God says in His book not to allow any unwholesome talk to come out of your mouth (Ephesians 4:29), then, with God's help, don't allow any unwholesome talk to come out of your mouth. Period. End of sentence. If God says in His book to abstain from sex outside of marriage (Hebrews 13:4), then don't sleep with your girlfriend, be unfaithful to your spouse, or fantasize to pornography on the Internet. It's that straightforward. If God says in His book to let go of bitterness toward those who've wronged you (Ephesians 4:31), or to return a minimal 10 percent of your income to the Lord's work (Malachi 3:10), or to honor your father and mother (Ephesians 6:1, 2), these are not optional suggestions for your consideration. This is God speaking to you. Authoritatively!

If you are ignoring God's Word, you are building your house on sand. And one day it's going to come crashing down. Let me encourage you, instead, to build your house on the rock-solid foundation of Scripture. Read the Bible daily. Join a small group and study the Bible with others. Take notes when you hear the Bible being taught at church—and don't miss a weekend service. Value the Bible's input over any advice that you get from a counselor or expert or friend. Let the Bible become your final authority.

Several months ago a husband and wife approached me after the church service, asking me to settle their dispute. The man had just lost his job. He had been an executive for a large company that was downsizing. He'd been given a very generous severance package. And that was the focus of the dispute with his wife. She felt that they should tithe on the severance (i.e., put 10 percent of it in the offering bag), since it was income the Lord had provided. And he was angry at the thought of doing any such thing. As he explained to me, executive positions are hard to find and so it would be irresponsible to give away some of the severance money that they might need to live on while he was job-hunting.

VALUE THE BIBLE'S input over any advice from an expert or friend. Let the Bible become your final authority.

The man wanted to know what I thought they should do. Even though I knew that my counsel might be suspect, since I'm the pastor of the church that would benefit from a tithe on his severance package, I still encouraged him to obey what the Bible says and return a portion of this income to the Lord. I said, "This is a time in your life when you can't afford for God to be sitting on the sidelines. You would welcome His participation by doing what His Word tells you to do."

To his credit, the guy went home and wrote out a tithe check. But that's not the end of the story. Within a week's time, four companies had called him for job interviews. He was back at work in short order. He saw that as a bit miraculous, and so did I. We both also made the connection between his submission to God's authority and God's blessing.

The Bible is *God's Autobiography*. As such, it is a supernatural, inerrant, and authoritative book. And you are a budding theologian, having just covered the critical *Doctrine of Inspiration*.

Study Guide

The *Study Guide* questions at the end of each chapter have been designed for your personal benefit. *All* questions can be used for personal study and, if you're part of a discussion group, for preparation for your group meeting. If you are part of a small group, you will find that the questions preceded by the group icon (😊) are especially useful for discussion. Your group leader can choose from among those questions when the group meets.

Icebreaker

What tall tale (i.e., frequently recounted and increasingly exaggerated personal story) has become well-known among your family or friends?

1. What is wrong with viewing the Bible's inspiration in terms of its *writers* or *readers*?

   According to 2 Timothy 3:16, what *is* it about the Bible that's inspired (i.e., God-breathed)? Practically speaking, what does this mean? How does God-*breathed* differ from God-*dictated*?

2. (icon) Describe a situation in which your belief that the Bible is *God's* Word was called into question or ridiculed. How did you defend your position at the time (or *did* you)?

3. (icon) List and briefly describe the six evidences that point to the supernatural character of the Bible. Which of these impresses you the most? Why?

4. Give three reasons for believing in the inerrancy of Scripture.

In what sense would refusing to believe in the Bible's inerrancy put you in a position of authority over Scripture?

5. How might you respond to someone who claims that the Bible is "full of errors"?

6. In what way(s) is the counsel of God's Word different from the counsel you receive from any other source (e.g., friend, therapist, self-help book, teacher, consultant, etc.)?

7. What is the basic difference between the guy who builds on rock and the one who builds on sand in Jesus' parable (Matthew 7:24–29)? Give some real-life examples of what could happen to you if you build on sand.

8. What step(s) might you take to ensure that you are building your life on rock?

9. Describe a time in your life (if you can) when obedience to some directive in God's Word brought you blessing.

{ 2 }

Lost in Transmission?

HAVE YOU EVER PLAYED the telephone game at a party? You know the basic setup. Everybody sits in a circle. One person is given a slip of paper with a sentence or two on it. He reads it to himself and then whispers what he's read into the ear of the person on his left. She then passes on what she thinks she's heard into the next person's ear.

Around the circle the phone message goes. By the time it reaches the last person, who completes the loop by saying the sentence out loud, it doesn't sound anything like the original statement.

Some skeptics of Christianity claim this is exactly what has happened with the transmission of the Bible. Whatever the Bible said when it was originally written was copied again and again and again over the years. And each time it was copied errors were introduced into the text. So what we read in the Bible today is a total distortion of what was originally written. Maybe you've heard this line of reasoning before.

In chapter 1, I drove home the point that the Bible is unlike any other book because its very words have been breathed out by God. Wow! But how do we know that what was breathed out by God was accurately passed along over the centuries? How do we know that it wasn't *lost in transmission* like the message that gets distorted as it goes around the circle in a game of telephone?

The Copying: *Hang Up the Phone Analogy!*

Let me begin by noting two basic problems with the telephone analogy. First, *the Bible's transmission has involved the careful copying of a written document*, not the whispered communicating of an oral message. Big difference!

To illustrate that difference, let's change the rules for the game of telephone. What if we handed out pencils and slips of paper and circulated the original message *in writing*? Each person would have to carefully copy the previous person's note before passing it on. Do you think this would improve the accuracy of the transmission? Of course it would! Well, this is how the Bible was transmitted. You say: "Well, somebody might still have become sloppy and miscopied a word." That's possible. But let me tell you how carefully the Bible was copied.

The last couple of times Sue and I were in Israel, we visited the site of the ancient Qumran community. This community thrived between 200 BC and AD 100 and it was responsible for producing the copies of the Bible that we know as the Dead Sea Scrolls. Here's what we've learned about how seriously these Bible copiers approached their task. For starters, they did their writing on specially prepared skins of clean (kosher) animals. Each skin was prepared to contain a certain number of columns. The spacing between consonants, sections, and books was precise—measured by threads. The ink had to be black and prepared according to a special recipe to ensure it would not fade.

There's more. No words could be written from memory. The transcriber had to have the manuscript he was copying right in front of him at all times. And copying the Bible was such an important task that the scribe would take a ritual bath and put on special clothes before sitting down to do it. Listen to this quotation from a first-century copier named Ishmael. He says to his fellow scribes, "Be careful in your work for it is the work of Heaven, lest you err either in leaving out or in adding one iota, and thereby cause the destruction of the whole world."[1]

No pressure, eh? You'll just destroy the world if you mess up your copying! These transcribers did their work as if the survival of the planet depended upon their accuracy. Clearly the careful copying of the written Scripture bears no resemblance to the frivolous whispering that goes on in a game of telephone.

There's a second reason why telephone is a lousy analogy for the Bible's transmission. To ensure quality control of the Bible's transmission, *copyists regularly compared manuscript copies with each other*. But this isn't how you play the game of telephone, is it?

Let's suppose there are ten people in your telephone circle. When person number five gets the message, whom does she get it from? (This is *not* a trick question.) She gets it from person number four. And that means (hang in there) that if person four miscommunicates the message, person five will pass that miscommunication on to person six. There's no way that person five can know to correct person four's error before passing on the message.

But what if we changed the rules of the game once again? What if person five is allowed to double-check the message she receives from person four, by asking persons one, two, and three for their input? Wouldn't that ensure accuracy in transmission?

That's what *does* happen today when Bible scholars reconstruct a document like the New Testament. They do it by comparing *all* the copies they have with each other. And it's estimated that there are up to 30,000 copies of the New Testament in existence. That allows for a lot of comparing!

Of course, all that comparing sometimes gives the Bible's detractors ammunition. A few years ago liberal Bible scholar

Bart Ehrman wrote a bestseller called *Misquoting Jesus*.[2] Dr. Ehrman is one of the world's leading textual critics of the New Testament. His book claims that readers can't trust the text of the New Testament today because there are between 200,000 and 400,000 variants (i.e., differences) among the manuscript copies that we have of the New Testament. Big problem, right? Dr. Ehrman thinks it is. That's why he says that any Bible you read today is most assuredly *misquoting Jesus*.

How do we respond to Ehrman? He's an expert. He's received a PhD in New Testament and teaches at a major university. He's written a popular book on this subject. Well, the best way to counter a so-called expert is with an opposing expert. And that's what Lee Strobel does in his book *The Case for the Real Jesus*. Strobel interviews Daniel Wallace on the topic of the New Testament's transmission.[3]

Dr. Wallace knows his Greek New Testament. In fact, he's written a textbook on Greek grammar that's currently being used by two-thirds of the schools that teach intermediate Greek, including Yale, Princeton, and Cambridge. Besides being a Greek expert, Wallace has studied the countless copies we have of the New Testament. He's even traveled around the world and taken more than 35,000 high-resolution digital photographs of the New Testament copies. They're posted on his website so that scholars can study them and compare them.

What does Wallace say about Ehrman's claim that there

are 200,000 to 400,000 variants among our copies of the New Testament? Wallace begins by pointing out that, since we have up to 30,000 copies of the New Testament, it's not surprising that we can find 200,000 to 400,000 variants among those copies. That averages to only ten variants per copy. Not a big deal. Furthermore, a close study of those variants reveals that between

UP TO 80 percent of text variants have to do with spelling differences, often the difference of just a single letter.

70 percent and 80 percent of them have to do with spelling differences, often the difference of just a single letter.

In addition, there are many cases in which the variant is due to the copier using a synonym. For example, one manuscript might read, "Jesus" said such and such, while other manuscripts read, "The Lord" said such and such. *Not* a huge difference. The fact is: only 1 percent of all the variants, according to Wallace, have any impact on the meaning of a text. And that impact is usually quite insignificant.

Thus the thousands of ancient copies of the New Testament that allow modern Bible scholars to compare manuscripts with each other ensure that today's New Testament is an accurate transmission of the original.

Great! But what about the copies we have of the Old

Testament? Do they also ensure an accurate transmission of the original? The answer rests in a special discovery found in several Middle East caves in 1947. That year, a shepherd boy (and subsequently archaeologists) discovered the Dead Sea Scrolls. At the time of their discovery the oldest copy we had of the Hebrew Old Testament dated back to about AD 900. But the Dead Sea Scrolls are copies of the Hebrew Old Testament that date back to 200 BC.

And you know what Bible scholars discovered when they compared the AD 900 copies with the 200 BC copies? Amazing agreement! Though these two sets of copies were separated by over a thousand years, the only variants were very minor. For example: in Isaiah 53, an important passage that prophesizes the coming of Christ and His death for our sins, there's only one word that's different between the AD 900 copies and the 200 BC copies.

Can the transmission of Old Testament manuscripts be trusted? Absolutely!

The trustworthiness of both the Old and New Testaments raises another important question, a more basic question that we now address.

The Canon: What Are the Right Books?

We've just learned that the sixty-six books of the Bible have been accurately copied over the centuries. But how do we know that scribes were copying the right books?

This question has to do with the canon of the Bible. Now, when I say *canon*, don't think boom-boom cannon—that's cannon with two *n*'s. The canon I'm talking about has only one *n*. *Canon* comes from a Greek word that means *measuring stick*. The canon of the Bible has to do with which books were accepted into the Bible (and which books were kept out). This canon was determined with the help of a measuring stick—certain standards that were used to decide which books were God-breathed and which ones were not.

Who Decides What's in and What's out?

Before we take a look at four of these standards, let me say a brief word about *who* determined the canon of the Old Testament and *who* determined the canon of the New Testament.

There are thirty-nine books in the Old Testament. The first, Genesis, was written by Moses about 1400 BC; the last, Malachi, by that prophet around 430 BC. All of the other Old Testament books were authored sometime during the thousand years between those two dates. So, how did they get collected into one volume? And who decided what was in and what was out?

Our information on the forming of the Old Testament canon is a bit sketchy, but according to Jewish tradition Ezra, a scholar and religious leader, played a huge role. Ezra helped

Israel to rebuild as a nation after many of its citizens had been released from a seventy-year Babylonian captivity. To be sure that God's people got restarted on the right foot, he put a lot of time into teaching them God's Word. But what *was* God's Word? Ezra set out to answer that question.

He pulled together a 120-person council of devout leaders, later referred to as the *Great Synagogue*. In 425 BC (just five years after Malachi completed the last book of the Old Testament), Ezra's council determined which books would comprise the Old Testament canon.

Just a footnote to this point: Even though not all Bible scholars agree that it was Ezra and his buddies who had the final say in establishing this canon, we do know that the canon must have been determined by the time of Jesus. By that time, Jesus occasionally referred to "the Scripture," indicating a standardized version of the Old Testament existed by then.

What about the New Testament canon? The New Testament is made up of twenty-seven books, beginning with the four Gospels, the biographies of Jesus. Who decided which books were in and which books were out for this portion of the Bible? And when was that decided?

Well, if you get your information from Dan Brown, the author of the best-selling mystery novel *The Da Vinci Code*[4] (which later became a Tom Hanks movie), the New Testament canon wasn't determined until AD 325 at the Council of

Nicaea. And that council was pulled together by the Roman Emperor Constantine, who was trying to unify his empire by forcing Christianity on everybody. Brown claims very conservative representatives dominated the council and chose only books for the New Testament canon that supported their narrow viewpoint that Jesus Christ was God. And they left out a lot of good stuff!

But Brown's conclusions are flagrantly wrong. For one thing, the first list we have of the New Testament's twenty-seven books dates all the way back to AD 170. That list is called the *Muratorian Fragment*. And besides the evidence of that list, historians tell us that the church was already using these particular twenty-seven books and *not* using other books, long before the Council of Nicaea met in AD 325. The only thing that this council did was to *formally* approve the twenty-seven books that the church had *informally* recognized for years as being God-breathed.

Brown also dismisses as ridiculous the belief among Christians that New Testament books are inspired by God simply because some church council included them in the canon. "C'mon!" Dan Brown would chide us: "One day Matthew's Gospel was just another ordinary biography of Jesus. And the next day it became 'inspired,' just because some church council canonized it?" But Brown is missing the point. Being canonized didn't *make* certain books inspired. Being canonized simply *recognized* these books as having been God-inspired. Do you see the difference?

Let me illustrate. Let's say I visit an antique store, buy an old painting, and take it home. When I go to reframe it, I discover another work of art on the back of it. In the corner it says: *Rembrandt*. I take it to an art dealer, an expert, and he does some tests on it after which he officially announces that my painting is indeed a Rembrandt. Here's my question: When did my

> **THE CHURCH councils didn't *make* the New Testament books God-inspired. They *recognized* books that were already God-inspired.**

Rembrandt become a Rembrandt? When Rembrandt painted it, right? It was a Rembrandt long before that art dealer recognized it as such. It didn't take his official recognition to make it a Rembrandt!

Similarly, Ezra and his buds didn't *make* the Old Testament books that they canonized God-inspired. The church councils in AD 300-and-something didn't *make* the New Testament books that they canonized God-inspired. All that canonization did was to *recognize* which books were already God-inspired and should thus be included in the Bible, God's Holy Word.

By the way, this is the reason why the Roman Catholic

Church is mistaken to assert that church tradition is of equal or greater authority than the Bible because church tradition gave us the Bible. No it didn't! *God* gave us the Bible. Church tradition only recognized which books had been God-inspired.

The Standards: *Gotta Pass These Tests!*

So what are those standards used to decide which books are God-breathed and which ones are not? The standards to measure inspiration of the manuscripts are really four tests.

First, there's the authorship test. I'll never forget a heated exchange that took place in the vice presidential debate of 1988 between Dan Quayle (Republican) and Lloyd Bentsen (Democrat). At the time, some people considered Quayle too young and inexperienced to be the vice president. So, in an effort to address this concern, while at the same time endearing himself to voters of both parties, Senator Quayle said: "I have as much experience as Jack Kennedy did when he sought the presidency." (JFK, of course, had been a very popular president.)

Senator Bentsen, a much older man than Quayle, retorted with these stinging words: "Senator, I served with Jack Kennedy. I knew Jack Kennedy. Jack Kennedy was a friend of mine." Then Bentsen paused before delivering the zinger. "And Senator, you are *no* Jack Kennedy!"[5] Whoa! Game, set, match. Here's the point of my story. The writers of the New

Testament books were all apostles or people who were closely associated with an apostle and so they had served with Jesus, they knew Jesus, they were friends of Jesus.

Back to Dan Brown, who claims that when the church chose to make Matthew, Mark, Luke, and John the official Gospels of the New Testament, they rejected eighty-some additional biographies of Jesus. Those were equally qualified, Brown says. Grant Osborne, who has a PhD in New Testament, responds that there were only about seventeen alternative gospels around when the books of Matthew, Mark, Luke, and John were canonized. *Not* eighty![6] Brown's claim is rubbish.

Those seventeen alternative gospels can all be dated between AD 150 and 300. In other words, they were written one to three *centuries* after Jesus. This obviously means that the writers of these alternative gospels could not have been personally familiar with Jesus any more than you and I could be personally familiar with someone who lived one to three hundred years ago. (How well, for example, could you possibly know Abraham Lincoln?)

But Matthew, Mark, and John *were* deeply familiar with Jesus. Matthew and John were members of Jesus' original band of twelve disciples. Mark, although not himself a disciple, got his information about Jesus from his close friend, Peter, who was another one of the original twelve. (In 1 Peter 5:13, Peter wrote that Mark was like a son to him.) And Luke got his information about Jesus from his ministry-partner, Paul, who'd had a real-life encounter with the risen Jesus on the road to Damascus. That's why the early church considered Paul to be an official apostle, even though he'd not been one of the Twelve. So all four Gospel writers had the personal scoop on Jesus.

Take a look at what one of them, Luke, says about his credentials for writing Jesus' biography: "Many have undertaken to draw up an account of the things that have been fulfilled among us, just as they were handed down to us by those who from the first were eyewitnesses and servants of the word" (Luke 1:1–2).

MATTHEW, MARK, Luke, and John *were* deeply familiar with Jesus. All four had the personal scoop on Jesus.

Note that Luke claims to be basing his biography of Jesus on eyewitness accounts. In fact, the word "eyewitnesses" is in the plural. Evidently, Luke not only got firsthand information about Jesus from the apostle Paul, he must have interviewed others as well. He interviewed people who had personally heard what Jesus said and seen what Jesus did.

That makes me wonder if one of those people whom Luke consulted for his biography was Mary, Jesus' earthly mother. The fact that Luke was a doctor, someone who would have had a professional interest in Mary's childbirth experience, may explain why he gives us more details about Jesus' birth than any other Gospel writer. I'm not suggesting that Luke was Mary's OB/Gyn doctor. I'm just saying that it wouldn't surprise me if he'd heard about Mary's labor and delivery from the mom herself.

So, Luke's Gospel passes the authorship test. And that's one of the reasons it was included in the New Testament, along with the Gospels of Matthew, Mark, and John. What about all the other books of the New Testament? They, too, are all tied to an apostle or to someone who was intimately familiar with Jesus. Hebrews is the only New Testament book that doesn't have a clear connection to an apostle. But for years Bible scholars associated it with the apostle Paul, which is why it initially passed the authorship test.

What's amazing about these New Testament authors is that early on their books were recognized as being on par with Old Testament Scripture. Look at what Peter says about the writings of the apostle Paul in this regard (2 Peter 3:16): "His letters [i.e., Paul's New Testament epistles] contain some things that are hard to understand, which ignorant and unstable people distort, as they do the other Scriptures." Did you catch that last phrase? Peter likens Paul's letters to Old Testament Scripture! That's more than a passing compliment. That's an incredible claim. Peter claimed Scripture status for Paul's writings.

What about the books of the Old Testament? What was the authorship test for their inclusion in

PETER LIKENS Paul's letters to Old Testament Scripture! Peter claimed Scripture status for Paul's writings.

the canon? Obviously, they weren't written by apostles, since apostles came much later. But they *were* written by prophets. Prophets were God's approved spokesmen. Moses, David, Isaiah—they were all considered prophets of one sort or another because God had put His words in their mouths. (See Exodus 4:10–12.)

I love the picturesque way that this happened in the life of Ezekiel. God appeared to Ezekiel in a vision, handed him a scroll, and told him to eat it (Ezekiel 3:3). Ezekiel records that the scroll tasted like honey to him. And when he finished the last bite, God said: "Go now to the house of Israel and speak my words to them" (v. 4). The Old Testament prophets were marked by God's *words*.

They were also marked by God's *power*. The prophets were accredited as God's spokesmen by supernatural signs that attended their ministries. All thirty-nine Old Testament books pass the *authorship test*. They were written by men who were recognized as prophets.

Second, there's the accuracy test. Back in 2004, when President George W. Bush was running for re-election, CBS News anchor Dan Rather got himself in deep weeds because of a story he aired on Bush. Reporting on the news magazine *60 Minutes,* Rather cited four memos that were supposedly written by Bush's National Guard commander back in 1972. These memos were extremely critical of Bush. They claimed that he had failed to complete his military service and that he had received special treatment because of his father's connections.

Rather made a big deal out of the authenticity of these memos. He even brought in a handwriting expert who vouched for the signature at the bottom of the notes.[7] Eventually, however, it turned out that the memos were phony— obviously phony. For starters, they had been created on Microsoft Word, not on a 1970s typewriter. (Oops!) And they had been supplied by a National Guardsman who publicly blamed President Bush for cutting his benefits. Four months later an independent panel concluded that CBS News failed to follow basic journalistic principles in the preparation and reporting of its broadcast.[8]

In the middle of this accuracy investigation came an amusing (and amazing) statement by Marian Carr Knox, the secretary to the commander of Bush's Air National Guard squadron who would have typed the documents. She told the *New York Times* she also believed the documents were fake but "the information in them is correct."[9] If you're a high school student, I don't recommend telling your history teacher, should she catch you turning in a forged research paper, "Well, the documents are fake but the information in them is accurate."

Accuracy *is* important, and the sixty-six books of the Bible had to pass the *accuracy test* in order to be included in the canon. Let's start with the Old Testament. I've already mentioned that the Old Testament's authors had to be recognized as prophets of God. And in order to be recognized as prophets of God, 100 percent of what they predicted had to come true. That's right, 100 percent! No room for one incorrect prophecy. Look at what Deuteronomy 18:21–22 says about this: "You may say to yourselves, 'How can we know when a message has not been spoken by the Lord?'

THE *ACCURACY* test was not graded on a curve. Old Testament prophets had to score 100 percent in order to pass.

If what a prophet proclaims in the name of the Lord does not take place or come true, that is a message the Lord has not spoken."

So the *accuracy test* was not graded on a curve. Those who professed to be Old Testament prophets had to score 100 percent in order to pass. Let me give you a quick example of how this played out. There are over one hundred prophecies in the Old Testament concerning the ancient city of Babylon. The prophet Jeremiah predicted that one day the city's walls would be leveled and never be rebuilt. Those walls were 187 feet thick and they encircled an area of almost two hundred square miles. Amazingly, those mighty walls eventually were destroyed—even though they were stronger and longer than the Great Wall of China, which still stands today. And Babylon has never been rebuilt. Alexander the Great declared plans to do so. But Alexander died shortly after making his announcement. The Bible's prophecies were right on the money.

That shows you the accuracy of an Old Testament prophecy. But what about the basic historical episodes that the Old Testament records? Are they trustworthy? Here's an example of accurate history. Up until 1993, many so-called Old Testament scholars doubted the historicity of King David. "It's true," they said, "that the Bible has a lot to say about this King of Israel, not to mention all those psalms that he supposedly wrote. But there's never been one shred of archaeological evidence to support the fact that David ever lived." Some liberal scholars have even gone so far as to say: "David's a myth, nothing but a legendary hero." Interestingly, I recently had a discussion about the Bible with a new friend, who is a well-read skeptic, and he raised this very issue with me.

Yet in 1993 archaeologists discovered some writings that date back to the ninth century BC, shortly after David's "imaginary" reign. Those writings described a military victory of a local king over "King David of the Israelites." So much for David's mythological status. Nobody dares to say today that David never existed (except doubters who are unfamiliar with the 1993 discovery).

What about the accuracy of the New Testament writers? Let's return to Luke 1 for a moment. Luke writes, "Therefore, since I myself have carefully investigated everything from the beginning, it seemed good also to me to write an orderly account for you, most excellent Theophilus, so that you may know the certainty of the things you have been taught" (vv. 3–4).

Luke claims to have "carefully investigated everything" that he's going to write about. And he says that his Gospel is going to be an "orderly account," the facts of which his readers could be *certain*.

Did Luke pass the accuracy test? Archaeologist John McRay, author of the textbook *Archaeology and the New Testament* and a regular consultant on TV networks for stories about archaeology and the Bible, concludes, "The general consensus of both liberal and conservative scholars is that Luke is very accurate as a historian."[10]

No doubt one of those scholars alluded to by Dr. McRay is Sir William Ramsay, who concedes Luke's accuracy. Ramsay, the son of atheists, and himself at one time an atheist, had a PhD from Oxford. Ramsay gave his whole life to archaeology, setting out to disprove the Bible. He arrived in the Holy Land with the

"THE GENERAL consensus of both liberal and conservative scholars is that Luke is very accurate as a historian."

particular goal of uncovering evidence that would discredit Luke's New Testament book of Acts. After twenty-five years of investigation, he became so impressed by the accuracy of Luke that he published a work stating that this portion of New Testament history is exact, down to the minutest details. He called Luke "a historian of the first rank. . . . This author should be placed along with the very greatest historians."[11] And to top it off, Ramsay shocked the whole scholarly world by declaring himself to be . . . a Christian!

Third, there's the alignment test. Remember the standardized tests that we took in grade school? I think they were used to measure our reasoning ability. There would be a picture of four items and we were asked to identify which of the four didn't go with the others. Remember? . . . "Mittens, scarf, hammer, and boots. Which one doesn't belong?" (I hope you're not struggling with this.) One of these four things is out of alignment with the other three. If you didn't identify the out-of-alignment item as the hammer, it's amazing that you got through grade school!

What does this have to do with the Bible's canon? Simple: The canonizers tended to include books in the Bible that seemed to fit well with other books that had already been recognized as God-breathed. And they tended to exclude books from the Bible that seemed to be questionable, incomplete, or just plain weird.

A perfect example of what I'm talking about is the apocryphal books. "Apocryphal" means "hidden," because these books were considered to be hidden from acceptance by the church for centuries. They weren't considered to be God-breathed. At least, not until 1546. (I'll explain what happened in 1546 in just a moment.) The apocryphal books were all written during the period between Old Testament times and New Testament times; between 200 BC and the first century; between the days of Malachi and the days of Matthew.

Several of these books have very interesting names: Tobit, Judith, Bel and the Dragon, 1 and 2 Maccabees, the Song of Three Young Men. Some of these books give us helpful historical insights into this time period. But some contain material that just doesn't seem to align with what is taught in the rest of the Bible. And that's why they weren't considered to be God-breathed until 1546 by the Roman Catholic Church.

Do you remember what was going on in the church during 1546? The Reformation! The Roman Catholic Church was being challenged. People were leaving the church in large numbers. The problem was corruption. A lot of questionable traditions had sprung up in the church, including the sale of indulgences for the purpose of raising money for church building projects. People were objecting: "Hey, where is some of this stuff in the Bible? What's the biblical rationale for practices such as buying a deceased loved one out of purgatory? Does the Bible even mention purgatory?"

The truth was that some of the church's doctrines at the time, such as purgatory, couldn't be traced back to the Bible. At least, not back to the thirty-nine books that Ezra and company had identified hundreds of years earlier as the God-breathed Old Testament, nor to the recognized books of the New Testament. Where *did* the doctrine of purgatory come from? From 2 Maccabees, one of the apocryphal books. So in 1546, at the Council of Trent, the Roman Catholic Church decided to add the apocryphal books to the Bible.

> THE APOCRYPHAL books are never quoted in the New Testament, while many of the Old Testament books are.

It's revealing to note that these books are never quoted in the New Testament, while many of the Old Testament books are. And there are only three apocryphal books that are found among the Dead Sea Scrolls, although copies of every Old Testament book except one are there (Esther). The apocryphal books don't pass the alignment test.

When it comes to the New Testament, this is why the alternative gospels (that Dan Brown loves) have been left out. There's just some weird stuff there. Now, I'm not talking about miracles, which, of course, are found in abundance in the four Gospels, written by Matthew, Mark, Luke, and John. There are instances of Jesus stilling storms, healing lepers, and feeding a crowd with five loaves and two fish. But there was an obvious purpose behind each of these miracles—to demonstrate the deity and compassion of Christ. They weren't random.

The rejected gospels, on the other hand, include stories like the one about Jesus as a toddler making birds of clay. When Jesus finished His sculpting, He clapped His hands and the clay birds flew away. What's the purpose of that random, frivolous act? Another rejected gospel, the Gospel of Peter, has Jesus stepping out of His tomb carrying the cross. (Don't ask me what the cross was doing in the tomb.) But that's not all. The cross talks! I'm not making this up.

And then there is some pretty strange teaching in these gospels-that-didn't-make-the-cut. Here are two of my favorite quotes from the Gospel of Thomas: "Blessings on the lion, if a human eats it, making the lion human. Foul is the human if a lion eats it, making the lion human."[12] Try applying that one to your life! This next one is even better:

Jesus said unto them, "When you make the two into one, and when you make the inner like the outer and the outer like the inner, and the upper like the lower, and when you make the male and female into a single one, so that the male will not be the male, nor the female be female, when you make eyes in the place of an eye, a hand in the place of a hand, a foot in the place of a foot, an image in the place of an image, then you will enter the Kingdom.[13]

Run that by me again. How does a person enter the kingdom? Crazy!

Now you understand why there was a need for an alignment test. Luke alludes to this alignment test in the very last phrase of the passage that we keep returning to in this chapter (Luke 1:1–4). Look at verse 4: "so that you may know the certainty of the things you have been taught." Luke is telling his readers that what he's about to present to them in his Gospel is going to back up the things that they have already been taught. In other words, Luke's Gospel is going to align with the rest of the Bible. Nothing weird about it.

Fourth, there's the acceptance test. I don't really need to say much about the acceptance test because nearly everything has already been said. The thirty-nine books that made it into the Bible's Old Testament canon were widely accepted by God's people. These books were found among the Dead Sea

Scrolls. They were quoted by Jesus and by the writers of the New Testament. And that can't be said for other writings, such as the apocryphal books.

Similarly, the twenty-seven books that made it into the Bible's New Testament canon were widely accepted by the church. These books weren't forced upon Christ followers by some church council that was bought and paid for by Emperor Constantine. Christ followers had already whittled down and were using the list of books that they believed were God-breathed.

Did I exhaust you with this study of the Bible's transmission? Well, I hope I also convinced you of the reliability of God's Word. That's important for our confidence and assurance for daily living. This Book can be trusted as a firm foundation for your life.

To watch Jim's midpoint comments about Foundation,
scan this QR code with your smartphone or go to
www.biblesavvy.com/video/#foundation2.

Study Guide

Icebreaker

Describe a favorite party or board game.

1. 👥 Why is the telephone game *not* a good analogy for how the Bible was passed down over the years?

2. Why should we *not* be alarmed by Dr. Bart Ehrman's claim that there are 200,000 to 400,000 variants in our ancient copies of the New Testament?

👥 Why do you think a book like Ehrman's *Misquoting Jesus* became a bestseller?

3. Who approved which books made it into the Old Testament and the New Testament?

4. Use the Rembrandt analogy to explain why these two councils did not *make* the approved books to be God's Word.

How does our understanding of this point impact our view of the Bible's authority?

5. List the four standards that were used in determining which books made it into the Bible and explain what is meant by each standard.

6. Next to each of standards 1–3, write out the phrase(s) from Luke 1:1–4 that supports it.

7. Why didn't the rejected gospels (which Dan Brown is so fond of) make it into the Bible?

From what you know of Mr. Brown and his novel, why do you think he is such proponent of the rejected gospels?

8. Why would historical inaccuracies do serious damage to the Bible's credibility?

9. 😃😃😃 Several examples of how Scripture passes the accuracy test are given in *Foundation*. Pick a favorite that you'll be able to remember when the topic of the Bible's historical reliability comes up in conversation. Write it down here.

10. Why did the Roman Catholic Church add the apocryphal books to the Bible at the Council of Trent in 1546? Why don't Protestants accept these books as Scripture?

11. 😃😃😃 What did you learn in this chapter that bolsters your confidence in the Bible?

{ 3 }

The Only Way to Know

ELWOOD DOWD HAS a six-foot three-inch best friend named Harvey. Nothing unusual about that—except that Harvey is a rabbit. An *imaginary* rabbit. So goes the storyline of Mary Chase's Pulitzer Prize winning play that was later made into a Hollywood movie. Jimmy Stewart, whom everybody knows as the star of *It's a Wonderful Life*, plays the role of Dowd.

Elwood is a wealthy, forty-year-old bachelor who spends a lot of his time philosophizing about life at the local bar. His drinking buddy is a make-believe rabbit named Harvey. (We never see Harvey in the movie, although Harvey's shadow appears on the movie's promotional poster.) Elwood is good-natured and harmless. In fact, he enjoys making other people happy. Even so, his sister, Veta, tries to get Elwood committed to a sanatorium. *He's nuts!* she figures. This is where the fun begins. Staff members at the mental hospital soon come to believe in Harvey the rabbit and Veta ends up in the sanatorium.

The message of the movie is obvious: *A little bit of fantasy never hurt anybody.* In fact, if you've got an imaginary friend who positively impacts your life and the lives of others—that's great! You're not crazy. I am sure that religious skeptics would apply a message like this to a belief in God. They view God as a fantasy, along the same lines as Harvey, the six-foot-tall rabbit. Go ahead and believe in him if that gets you through the day. But he's not *real.* Or is he?

The Bible argues that God *is* real and that He has revealed Himself to us in its pages. The Bible claims to be the definitive source of information about God. While it is not our only source of information about Him, it is the only way to know Him deeply and personally. The Bible is where we go to learn about God's attributes, His plan of salvation, and His will for our lives. That is the focus of this chapter—what theologians refer to as the *Doctrine of Revelation.*

God's Attributes

A while back I was shopping at the grocery store when I ran into a woman whom I'd seen at one of our church's special events. A friend had brought her to Christ Community. When I inquired as to whether she'd enjoyed her visit, she responded enthusiastically with "I loved it!" So I asked her if she had any plans to return for one of our regular weekend services. Very politely, she declined, saying: "My husband and I have our own ideas about God." Although I hear lines like this all the time, they always leave me shaking my head.

"I have my own ideas about God." Is that allowed? Are we permitted to make up whatever we want to about God? Does God then become, in reality, what we imagine Him to be? This approach to God strikes me as so ridiculous that I want to shake people by the shoulders and declare: "You can't do that!" (So far, I've been able to suppress this impulse.) What makes people think that they can base their knowledge of God on their own ideas? Would you want people to come by their knowledge of *you* in this way?

Imagine this: You're at work, and you overhear two people talking in the office cafeteria. To your surprise, they're talking about you. Your ears prick up the moment you hear your name. They mention certain personality traits of yours, your likes and dislikes, your vocational goals, the causes that you're passionate about. But here's what's weird about the information they're throwing around—you've never talked with either one of them. They're making all this stuff up. They didn't get their insights about you from *you*. Wouldn't that drive you crazy?

People do that all the time with God. They surmise what He's like. One of the best-selling novels of recent years is *The Shack*. It's the account of a grieving dad who encounters God after his daughter has been murdered. The triune God appears in the book as a large African woman with a great sense of humor (God the Father), a laid-back handyman who likes to skip stones (God the Son), and a slight, young Asian woman (God the Spirit).

The author of this novel, in numerous interviews, has said that this is just his way of communicating what *he* thinks God is like. And millions of people who have read *The Shack* believe that they've gained a greater understanding of who God is through the book. I contend that this is sheer nonsense. We don't get to know God through *speculation* (whether that of a best-selling author or our own). The only way to truly know Him is through *revelation*—His disclosure of Himself to us.

There are two major sources of this revelation. They are vividly described in Psalm 19. C. S. Lewis, who taught literature at both Oxford and Cambridge, called this psalm "the greatest poem in the Psalter and one of the greatest lyrics in the world."[1] Take a look at the opening nine verses of Psalm 19 and see if you can identify the two major ways by which God reveals Himself to us:

> The heavens declare the glory of God; the skies
>   proclaim the work of his hands.
> Day after day they pour forth speech; night after night
>   they display knowledge.
> There is no speech or language where their voice is not
>   heard.

Their voice goes out into all the earth, their words to the
ends of the world.

In the heavens he has pitched a tent for the sun,
which is like a bridegroom coming forth from his
pavilion, like a champion rejoicing to run his course.
It rises at one end of the heavens and makes its circuit
to the other; nothing is hidden from its heat.

The law of the Lord is perfect, reviving the soul.
The statutes of the Lord are trustworthy, making wise
the simple.
The precepts of the Lord are right, giving joy to the
heart.
The commands of the Lord are radiant, giving light to
the eyes.
The fear of the Lord is pure, enduring forever.
The ordinances of the Lord are sure and altogether
righteous.

King David, the author of Psalm 19, begins his poem in
praise of how God reveals Himself to us in creation. David is
especially interested in what the sky has to say, whether it's
the stars that shine at night or the sun that blazes during the
day. These aspects of creation have a voice of their own. Just

look at all the verbs that David uses to describe creation's effort to communicate with us about God: *declare; proclaim; pour forth speech; display knowledge.*

The apostle Paul, no doubt with the opening lines of Psalm 19 running through his mind, makes a similar statement about the way in which creation reveals God to us: "What may be known about God is plain to them, because God has made it plain to them. For since the creation of the world God's invisible qualities—his eternal power and divine nature—have been clearly seen, being understood from what has been made" (Romans 1:19–20).

So, according to Paul, certain attributes of God, such as His *eternal power* and His *divine nature*, are revealed to us when we walk outside and look up

CERTAIN ATTRIBUTES of God are revealed to us when we walk outside and look up at the sky (or at the oceans, the mountains, the flowers).

at the sky (or at the birds, the oceans, the mountains, the flowers, or anything else that God has made). This is a wonderful truth. But it comes to us with a caveat. It is possible to gaze at the stars on a clear summer night and not conclude anything at all about God. Lots of people do this. Many are able to enjoy the stars, in fact, who deny the very existence of God. That is because creation speaks to us in a somewhat subtle voice. And even when her voice *is* heard, the information she gives us about God is not very specific. The attributes of His that she declares are rather generic.

If we are to know God in an intimate fashion, we need a revelation from Him that is more specific. Let me illustrate the value of a more explicit disclosure. Suppose that you're walking down a deserted beach one day. You see countless patterns in the sand that have been made by waves, by wind, by debris, and by sand crabs. But suddenly you come across some writing. It says: "Jason loves Lauren." You would immediately conclude a couple of things from that inscription. Not only would you deduce that a young man named Jason had recently been on this stretch of the beach (because there is no way that such writing got there by chance), you would also know something very particular about Jason: *he's wild about Lauren!*

God wants to disclose particulars about Himself to us. How does He do this? Let's go back to Psalm 19 and take a closer look at the second half of David's poem. After declaring that creation reveals God to us in broad brushstrokes, David makes a sharp right turn and begins to talk about a second, more specific form of revelation: God's Word. David's move from creation to Scripture is so abrupt that various liberal Bible scholars surmise that this psalm must actually be a compilation of two different poems, which some editor clumsily put together. But such reasoning totally misses the fact that there is a unifying, main point to Psalm 19. The main point is that God reveals Himself to us.

This revelation takes two forms, described in the two halves of Psalm 19. The first is creation. The second is the Bible, referred to by David as *laws*, *statutes*, *precepts*, *commands*, and *ordinances*. These two forms of revelation are closely tied together in David's psalm. While

GOD USES A second form of revelation . . . because it takes words to convey specifics.

creation's sun, for example, is known for giving light to the world and sustaining physical life (v. 6), so God's Word is capable of *giving light to the eyes* (v. 8) and *reviving the soul* (v. 7).

Theologians are fond of speaking of creation as God's *general* revelation and of Scripture as God's *special* revelation. Another way that it has been put is that creation is the "Big Book" about God and the Bible is the "Little Book" (little in size, that is, not in terms of all it communicates). Why is a second form of revelation necessary? Because it takes words to convey specifics. Without God's written Word, we'd be left with only the general impressions about God that are observable in nature. It is worth noting that David uses the *generic* name for God (Hebrew *El*, from *Elohim*) in the first half of his psalm when he's talking about creation's revelation, but switches to the *personal* name for God (Hebrew *Yahweh*) when he turns to Scripture's revelation.

Words convey personal details. Just as the writing in the sand told us that *Jason loves Lauren*, so the Bible tells us that God loves us—something that we would not have been able to deduce from creation alone. And love is not the only attribute of God that we find in the Bible. There are over 250 names, titles, and character traits in Scripture that describe God. Over 250! (In my first book, *Prayer Coach*, I include this list as an appendix so that readers can be specific when praising God in prayer.) If we want to know God—really know God—then we must make it our goal to discover all that He reveals about Himself in His Word.

God's Salvation

My good friend Nick Perrin is a New Testament scholar. Nick sure didn't see his vocation coming as he was growing up. Raised in a family of agnostics, none of the Perrins ever entered a church. But his mom and dad were very smart and wanted Nick to be very smart, so they sent him to a New England prep school during his high school years. Nick discovered he was pretty good at languages, taking Latin for four years.

In the summer before his senior year, he decided to try his hand at Greek. (Isn't this what all high school students do during their summer break?) He bought a Greek grammar book and began to master the basic rules. Once he had these under his belt, he looked for something to translate. The school was holding a used book sale, and Nick managed to pick up a copy of the Greek New Testament. He began in the Gospel of Mark, slowly translating one word at a time. In spite of the tediousness of the process, Nick became enthralled with the person of Jesus Christ. Shortly thereafter, he became a Christian. And years later, Nick Perrin is now a New Testament scholar. (By the way, I borrowed the title for the previous chapter, *Lost in Transmission?* from a book that Nick wrote on the same subject.[2] His writing is extremely engaging and I would highly recommend his book to those who want more information about how God has safeguarded the Bible from errors over the centuries of its transmission.)

There are many people like Nick, who have come to faith in Jesus Christ by simply reading the Bible. Mark Driscoll is another intriguing example. Mark was raised in a home behind a strip club in a rough neighborhood near Seattle. In his youth, he attended a Roman Catholic church where he served as an altar boy. But he gave up on "religion" as he got older. One day, as a college student, he picked up a Bible and started reading Paul's epistle of Romans. Gradually he began to understand the difference between religion and a personal relationship with Christ. Five years after surrendering his life to Jesus, Mark began Mars Hill Church where thousands of people now worship in Seattle and at satellite churches.

GOD USES His Word to point people to the salvation that is found in His Son.

You get the idea. God uses His Word to point people to the salvation that is found in His Son, Jesus Christ. This is how Timothy, to whom Paul wrote two New Testament epistles, came to faith. Paul reminds Timothy of "how from infancy you have known the holy Scriptures, which are able to make you wise for salvation through faith in Christ Jesus" (2 Timothy 3:15). The backstory is that Timothy was raised in a home where his dad was probably not a believer, but his mom and grandmother were. (See Acts 16:1 and 2 Timothy 1:5.) It's not hard to imagine Timothy's mom, Eunice, faithfully sharing the good news of Jesus with her son by reading the Bible to him.

Keep in mind that the Bible in Timothy's home would have been just the Old Testament. And yet there was plenty of information in this BC-dated book about a coming Savior. The Old Testament describes this Savior as a descendant of Eve (i.e., a human) who would defeat Satan, as a descendant of Abraham who would bring blessing to all peoples, as a prophet who would be greater than Moses, as a king who would reign on David's throne, and as a sacrificial lamb who would pay the penalty for people's sins with His death. This Savior turned out to be Jesus, as Timothy's mom would have explained to her son.

The Old Testament pointed so clearly to Jesus that Jesus Himself cited verses from it as proof that He was God's promised Savior. He told one group of religious listeners: "You diligently study the Scriptures because you think that by them you possess eternal life. These are the Scriptures that testify about me" (John 5:39).

On another occasion, shortly after Jesus' resurrection, He spoke with a couple of followers who were disillusioned by His crucifixion and not yet aware that He'd risen from the dead (nor that it was the resurrected Jesus who was speaking to them). Jesus "said to them, 'How foolish you are, and how slow of heart to believe all that the prophets have spoken! Did not the Christ have to suffer these things and then enter his glory?' And beginning with Moses and all the Prophets, he explained to them what was said in all the Scriptures concerning himself" (Luke 24:25–27).

Paul too used the Old Testament to point people to Christ. In city after city that he visited, he made a beeline for the local synagogue where "he reasoned with them from the Scriptures, explaining and proving that the Christ had to suffer and rise from the dead" (Acts 17:2–3). Paul proclaimed Jesus to be this Christ.

When Paul was later on trial for his faith before King Agrippa, he again referred to the Old Testament, declaring: "I am saying nothing beyond what the prophets and Moses said would happen—that the Christ would suffer and, as the first to rise from the dead, would proclaim light to his own people and to the Gentiles" (Acts 26:22–23). Even in Paul's final incarceration, "from morning till evening he explained and declared to them [i.e., large numbers of visitors] the kingdom of God and tried to convince them about Jesus from the Law of Moses and from the Prophets" (Acts 28:23).

The Bible, Old Testament as well as New, reveals to us God's Savior and His plan of salvation. Without the Bible we would be spiritually lost. Consider some of the specific truths that God's Word spells out regarding our need for salvation, truths without which we wouldn't have a clue about how to begin a relationship with God.

Sin's Consequences

For starters, the Bible explains that we have a very serious problem: *sin*. And our sin keeps a Holy God at a great distance. "For all have sinned and fall short of the glory of God" (Romans 3:23). "Your iniquities have separated you from your God; your sins have hidden his face from you, so that he will not hear" (Isaiah 59:2).

All this talk about sin, of course, raises the question: What is sin? Without a definition of such, we might be able to convince ourselves that we're not really that bad. That our own wrongdoing is the insignificant, harmless, garden variety kind. Here again, the Bible proves indispensable, because it spells out God's moral laws, which we regularly transgress, thus becoming clearly guilty of sin. As the apostle Paul says in Romans 7:7, he would not have known that coveting was a sin unless God's law had identified it as such. So the Bible defines sin before warning us that sin alienates us from God.

Unfortunately, the bad news gets worse. The Bible tells us that if something is not done about our sinful alienation from God, we will suffer the consequences of death. "The wages of sin is death. . . . The soul who sins is the one who will die . . . You will die in your sin" (Romans 6:23; Ezekiel 18:4; John 8:21). And as the Bible talks about death as a consequence for our sins, it presents a picture that includes spiritual, physical, and eternal death (see Ephesians 2:1 and 1 John 5:11–12.) Without God's Word, we would be naïve to this dreadful danger.

The Bible's Good News

Thankfully, the Bible also tells us that we can be rescued from our awful predicament. Jesus Christ, God's Son, was sent to earth to bear the penalty that our sins deserved. He suffered death on our behalf:

> For Christ died for sins once for all, the righteous for the unrighteous, to bring you to God. (1 Peter 3:18)

God demonstrates his own love for us in this: While we were still sinners, Christ died for us. (Romans 5:8)

He was pierced for our transgressions, he was crushed for our iniquities; the punishment that brought us peace was upon him, and by his wounds we are healed. We all, like sheep, have gone astray, each of us has turned to his own way; and the Lord has laid on him the iniquity of us all. (Isaiah 53:5–6)

This is good news. The best news in the world! But knowing all this, we would still be spiritually lost if it were not explained to us how we could tap into what Christ has done. How do we access the salvation that He purchased on the cross? Does God give it as a reward to those who measure up to a certain standard, or who live by the Golden Rule, or who go to church and participate in religious rituals, or who stay out of deep moral weeds? No! Once again, the Bible comes through with the necessary information, explaining that salvation is not acquired through personal efforts but by putting our faith in Jesus Christ as Savior and Lord:

For it is by grace you have been saved, through faith—and this not from yourselves, it is the gift of God—not by works, so that no one can boast. (Ephesians 2:8–9)

However, to the man who does not work but trusts God who justifies the wicked, his faith is credited as righteousness. (Romans 4:5)

If you confess with your mouth, "Jesus is Lord," and believe in your heart that God raised him from the dead, you will be saved. For it is with your heart that you believe and are justified, and it is with your mouth that you confess and are saved. (Romans 10:9–10)

I [Jesus] tell you the truth, whoever hears my word and believes him who sent me has eternal life and will not be condemned; he has crossed over from death to life. (John 5:24)

Clearly the Bible plays an indispensable role in revealing God's salvation to us. There is no way that we could figure out how to be saved without the input and clear direction of God's Word. That's why I wince every time I hear someone who is attempting to present God's offer of salvation to others but who is not using a generous amount of Scripture to do so.

Thirty years ago as a youth pastor, I brought a special speaker to a junior high retreat, a former Air Force pilot during the Vietnam War. For forty-five minutes on the first night he regaled us with stories about the dangerous missions he had flown. A hundred middle schoolers, jacked up on Mountain Dew and s'mores, listened spellbound to these tales of adventure.

At the end of his talk, the heroic pilot abruptly asked the students to bow their heads and raise their hands if they wanted to begin a relationship with Jesus Christ. Scores of hands punched the air. But afterward I quickly learned that most of these kids had no idea what they were signing up for. They just wanted to experience some of the same excitement that the speaker had radiated.

People don't come to Christ for salvation—not genuinely—simply on the basis of having heard someone's moving story. Nor do vague invitations to "become a follower of Jesus" or "experience God's love and forgiveness" result in true conversions if they are not preceded by a thorough, biblical explanation of what salvation is all about. Without the Bible, we would be left in the fog regarding God's salvation.

> **WITHOUT THE Bible, we would be left in the fog regarding God's salvation.**

This is why it's so important, when talking with others who are investigating the faith, to use a tool that explains salvation with a generous supply of Scripture verses. I personally like to scribble out a diagram, affectionately dubbed "The Bridge Illustration" by those who use it, on any available scrap of paper or napkin. It pictorially shows how we are separated from God by the chasm of our sins; none of our personal efforts to traverse the chasm work; Christ's cross bridged the chasm; and we can move across that bridge by putting our faith in Christ. These truths are all backed up with Bible verses, such as the ones that I quoted above.

I know that a tool like "The Bridge" strikes some people as being a bit canned. But I can tell you, from my own experience, that it's been immeasurably helpful in explaining God's plan of salvation to my friends. In fact, I know of at least two guys, now Christ followers, who still carry around in their wallets the copy of this diagram that I sketched for them on a napkin in some coffee shop years ago. Because it led them to salvation! (And if you are artistically challenged, don't feel like you need to be able to draw a diagram. Just start using one of the many small booklets, such as Billy Graham's *Steps to Peace with God* or the Navigators' "The Bridge to Life" illustration,[3] that explains salvation in simple terms to seekers with the help of Bible verses.)

God's Will

Some time ago, the title of a book by a well-known Christian author and speaker caught my eye. It promised to teach readers "the best question" that they could ever ask themselves when facing big decisions. To be honest, I initially tried to find out what the magic question was without buying the book. I skimmed the back cover, the introduction, and the first couple of chapters in search of it. But this writer did a pretty good job of hiding the question so that people like me would be forced to fork out the money for the book and read it cover to cover.

I'm going to do you a huge favor and give you that question for free. Here it is: *What is the wise thing to do?* I think that's a fantastic question to ask ourselves when trying to determine what direction to take as we stand at a crossroads. But there's one basic problem we're going to face in trying to use it. The question assumes that we're wise enough to figure out what the wise thing to do is.

You may have to read that last sentence a few times in order to catch its point. Maybe this would help. Imagine that you're stuck while taking a multiple-choice test at school. Would it be beneficial to ask yourself: *What's the smart answer to this question?* Wouldn't you have to *be* smart in order to know which answer is the smart one?

How do we become wise in the first place, so that when we ask ourselves, *What is the wise thing to do?* we will be able to answer our own question? Unfortunately, although the author of the book told his readers to address their concerns to God and fully submit to His leading—good advice—he didn't provide much instruction beyond that about how to become a wise person.

But, good thing for us, the apostle Paul explains how ordinary people can acquire indispensable savvy. Look at what Paul writes, just after reminding Timothy that it was the Bible that first introduced him to God's salvation: "All Scripture is God-breathed and is useful for teaching, rebuking, correcting and training in righteousness, so that the man of God may be thoroughly equipped for every good work" (2 Timothy 3:16–17).

If this passage sounds familiar, it's because in chapter 1 we camped out on it when we considered the inspiration of Scripture. The Bible is a supernatural book, you'll recall, because it is *God-breathed*. But having made this point, Paul now tells us what it means, practically speaking, for our lives. Paul informs us how to put the Bible to good use in our daily experience. Note carefully the four gerunds (*-ing* words) in verse 16: *teaching, rebuking, correcting,* and *training.*

Bible scholars tell us that these four action words fall into two neat categories. The first two action words describe the Bible's impact on our beliefs. It *teaches* us sound doctrine (i.e., truths about God and His ways) and it *rebukes* any erroneous thinking of ours. The second two words address the Bible's impact on our behavior. The Bible *corrects* any misconduct and *trains* us to act in a God-pleasing manner. The end result of all this input from God's Word is that we are "equipped for every good work."

This is the recipe for becoming a wise person that we've been looking for! The Bible is able to shape our beliefs and our

THE BIBLE is able to shape our beliefs and our behaviors so that we become wise people.

behaviors so that we become people whose lives are marked by fruitful service to God—wise people. And wise people are able to make wise decisions. They are able to answer the question: *What is the wise thing to do?*

Sometimes the answer to that question will be explicit in the Bible. Some verse will very directly say, regarding the decision you are facing, *Do this* or *Don't do that.* But even when the Bible does not clearly address the specifics of your situation, it will still prepare you to make a wise decision by making you a wise person.

Should you put your aging parent in a nursing home? There's no verse in the Bible that says yes or no to that. What should your major be in college? There's no verse that says *biology* or *literature* or *business.* Should you take the job transfer that offers more money but requires relocating your family to a new city? There's no verse that says to stay put or move to Denver. However, if you are saturating your life with God's Word, you will be able to make wise decisions in cases like these because you will be a wise person.

The key is to saturate your life with God's Word. Begin

now. Don't wait until you're staring an important but daunting decision in the face. You won't be able to become wise in that instant. You will already be wise or not be wise, depending on how much time you've been investing in your Bible. I think it was the great nineteenth-century preacher Charles Spurgeon who said that we should immerse ourselves in Scripture until our blood becomes *bibling*. I like that.

At the end of a recent football season, my Chicago Bears were embroiled in an intense play-off game. Unfortunately, our starting quarterback was injured and had to be replaced by his backup. It got worse. The second string quarterback got hurt and had to be replaced by our third-stringer. As the camera zoomed in on this guy just before he left the bench to jog onto the football field, he was frantically studying the playbook! I laughed out loud and shouted at my TV screen: "It's too late, pal. Game on! If you don't know the plays by now, you're in a heap of trouble!"

The same thing could be said of our personal lives. If we're suddenly faced with a big decision and desperately want to know God's will for our lives, frantically flipping through the Bible for explicit directions will probably not yield favorable results. However, if we are becoming wise people by constant exposure to God's Word, we will most likely make wise decisions.

As noted in this chapter, the Bible *reveals* to us God's

attributes, God's salvation, and God's will. This is a summary of what theologians are referring to when they talk about the doctrine of *revelation*.

Study Guide

Icebreaker

What guidelines do you think people should follow when providing information about themselves on Facebook? Is social media a good tool for getting to know other people? Why or why not?

1. When it comes to knowing who God is, what's the difference between *speculation* and *revelation*?

    Why is "I have my own ideas about God" such a ridiculous statement?

2. What are the two main sources of revelation about God? Why is the second source necessary?

What would you say to the guy who doesn't think that listening to a preacher in a church on Sunday is necessary since he can connect with God out in nature on his bass boat?

3. What specific truths about salvation are important for a spiritual seeker to understand? Next to each truth put a Bible verse or two that affirms that truth.

4. What is the danger in not using Scripture when presenting the gospel to someone?

5.  Have you found a booklet that has helped you communicate God's plan of salvation to others? If yes, what do you like about it? If no, how could you get your hands on such a resource this week?

 What are the benefits and liabilities of using a tool like this?

6. Why is it *not* helpful to ask yourself the question, *What is the wise thing to do?* when trying to make an important decision?

7. How does the Bible equip you to make wise decisions?

(icon) What is a big decision that you are currently faced with? What Bible verses (that you can think of) might help you with this decision—either by speaking to it directly, or by laying out principles for you to consider?

8. (icon) What specific steps could you take to ensure that you are moving in the direction of becoming Bible-wise?

{ **4** }

Get a Grip

ACCORDING TO A RECENT study by the U.S. Department of Education, almost half of all American adults have difficulty reading. To be exact, 43 percent are reading at a "basic" or "below basic" level.[1] "Basic" means that these adults could find their favorite sitcom listed in *TV Guide* but would have trouble reading the newspaper. The newspaper!

Reading is becoming a lost art for many people—especially young people. Less than one-third of thirteen-year-olds read on a daily basis, a 14 percent decline from twenty years ago.[2] Fifteen- to twenty-four-year-olds spend about seven minutes of their daily leisure time reading. That's less time than it takes them to pick up a latte at Starbucks.[3]

So what is everybody doing with the time that people used to invest in reading? You could probably guess the correct answer to that question, right? Those fifteen- to twenty-four-year-olds who read for a whopping seven minutes each day are watching two hours of TV. And television is only the tip of the iceberg when it comes to media distractions. Let's scroll through a few more of the alternatives to books.

There's the iPod (or similar mp3 players). Four of every five teens (79 percent) own one.[4] Apple sold more than 100 million iPods in the first five years.[5] There is the cell phone—not just for calling but for texting and tweeting. I recently read in my news magazine an article entitled "The Twitter Revolution." The second line of the article asked the question: "Is Twitter a breakthrough in personal communication or a colossal waste of time?"[6] Well, if it's a colossal waste of time, there are a lot of time-wasters out there, from the president of the United States to Martha Stewart. Everybody's tweeting!

Another big distraction from traditional reading is the Internet. In his book *The Shallows: What the Internet Is Doing to Our Brains*, technology writer Nicholas Carr concludes the Internet is making us stupid. He's got scientific research to back him up.[7] Studies show that jamming our brains with all sorts of data, from pop-up windows to hyperlinks, causes our memories to malfunction. We don't retain *anything*. What's the antidote? Carr says that reading books stretches our minds and improves our memories.

Still another alternative to reading good books is Facebook. One of every twelve people on the planet has a Facebook account today. At one point, an average of 700,000 new accounts were opened every day,[8] which is why *Time* magazine named Mark Zuckerberg, Facebook's founder, its "Person of the Year" in 2010. By fall 2012, Facebook announced they had more than one billion people who logged in each month.[9] How much time do you spend Facebooking these days?

Why am I making a big deal about the way in which modern media are minimizing the time that we spend reading good books? Because God's primary way of communicating with us is through a book—the Bible. If we are not voracious readers of God's book, our relationship with God and our spiritual growth are going to be seriously stunted. Which is why I am going to challenge you in this chapter to get into the Bible. Don't wait for the movie!

How to Get the Bible into Our Lives

Thus far in *Foundation* we have focused on how *God* authored the Bible, how *God* protected the accurate transmission of the Bible over hundreds of years, and how *God* reveals Himself and His will for our lives through the Bible. Do you see a pattern in these topics? The spotlight has been on God. We've been studying *His* role in the communication process. But now we're going to focus on *our* responsibility. How do we take full advantage of this book that God has given us? How do we get the Bible into our lives?

Reading is obviously a big part of it, because books

require reading. But we're going to look at three additional activities, besides reading, that will enable us to *get a grip* on the Bible. And speaking of getting a grip on the Bible, here's a little experiment. Of course, you'll need your own Bible to participate in this exercise. First, hold your Bible with your thumb and one finger. Not too hard to do, eh? OK, now I want you to hold your Bible with two fingers. That's better, but it's still not much of a grip, is it? It would be easy for the Bible to slip out of your grasp. Now try a three-finger grip . . . a four-finger grip.

It doesn't feel like you've got a really firm grip on your Bible until you're holding it with your thumb and all four fingers, right? What's my point? I'm about to give you five activities that will enable you to get a firm grip on God's book, the Bible. Don't settle for one or two of these activities. Begin, as soon as possible, to practice all five. (By the way, I learned the importance of these five activities years ago from the Navigators ministry. They specialize in getting people into God's Word and are known for their diagram of a five-finger grip on the Bible.[10])

Get a Grip on Scripture by Hearing

We're going to pitch our tents in Nehemiah 8 in this chapter, so you might want to open your Bible to that passage. The year is about 430 BC, and God's people have recently returned from seventy years of captivity in Babylon. Their country is a mess. The walls of their capital city, Jerusalem, and their once-beautiful temple are both heaps of rubble. The people are demoralized. They fully realize that the reason for their years of exile was because they'd wandered from God. So they want to be sure that this doesn't happen again.

How could they get their lives turned around and on the right track? Instinctively they know that it's time to start listening to God. They are eager to *hear* God's Word. So they call on their spiritual leader, a guy named Ezra, to read God's book to them.

Remember Ezra? In chapter 2 we described how Ezra and 120 of his buds—a group later referred to as the *Great Synagogue*—determined which thirty-nine books made it into the Old Testament. Now let's read what happened as God's people gather to hear the Bible read by Ezra upon their return from exile:

All the people assembled as one man in the square before the Water Gate. They told Ezra the scribe to bring out the Book of the Law of Moses, which the Lord had commanded for Israel.

So on the first day of the seventh month Ezra the priest brought the Law before the assembly, which was made up of men and women and all who were able to understand. He read it aloud from daybreak till noon as he faced the square before the Water Gate in the presence of the men, women and others who could understand. And all the people listened attentively to the Book of the Law.

Ezra the scribe stood on a high wooden platform built for the occasion. . . . Ezra opened the book. All the people could see him because he was standing above them; and as he opened it, the people all stood up. Ezra praised the Lord, the great God; and all the people lifted their hands and responded, "Amen! Amen!" Then they bowed down and worshiped the Lord with their faces to the ground.

The Levites . . . instructed the people in the Law while the people were standing there. They read from the Book of the Law of God, making it clear and giving the meaning so that the people could understand what was being read. (Nehemiah 8:1–8)

Wow! These people really wanted to *hear* God's Word. The opening verses tell us that *everybody* gathered to listen— men, women, and children who were old enough to understand. And they listened, Scripture says, "from daybreak till noon" (v. 3). What is that, about five to six hours? All that time they listened "attentively" (circle the word "attentively" in your Bible). Please note, too, the reverent way in which they listened. We're told that they bowed down and worshiped God before listening to Ezra read from God's book; then they stood to their feet and remained standing the entire time that they listened. That's reverence!

One last observation, here: Ezra and his Levite pals (all members of the priesthood) didn't just *read* the Bible to God's people. They *explained* it. The leaders were "making it clear and giving the meaning so that the people could understand what was being read." So, the people weren't just hearing Bible-*reading*, they were hearing Bible-*teaching*.

How do we become people of God's book? How do we begin to get a grip on the Bible? For starters, we must *hear* God's Word taught. Let me give you a few tips with respect to *hearing* God's Word.

First, listen with regularity. This was the top priority of the early church. Acts 2 tells us that after Jesus rose from the dead and ascended back to heaven, Peter stood up in Jerusalem and preached a sermon about Jesus. Three thousand people responded, repenting of their sins and putting their faith in Christ (v. 41). What did they do next? These brand-new Christ followers immediately "devoted themselves to the apostles' teaching" (v. 42). The word *devoted* means to do something with regularity and determination, to stick to it. What were they sticking to? Listening to their spiritual leaders teach them God's Word.

Is this something that you're devoted to? Making it to church one or two weekends a month is not devotion. If you are new to attending church, a couple of times a month may seem like a huge commitment. But it's not enough to give you a firm grip on God's Word. You'll end up missing a good deal of what your pastor is teaching. Make it your goal to listen with regularity by getting to church every weekend.

LISTEN WITH regularity, discernment, a pen in hand . . . and with the aim of putting what you hear into practice.

And on the rare occasion that you have to miss, listen to the teaching online if your church has a website that offers downloadable sermons.

Second, listen with discernment. I always cringe when I hear a sermon that is Bible-lite. You know what I mean by Bible-lite? Bible-lite sermons are constructed like skyscrapers (sorry about the coming pun): one story on top of another. Unfortunately, people love this kind of sermon, because it's funny, it's entertaining, it's emotionally moving. But it won't strengthen your grip on God's Word.

Make sure that you are attending a church whose pastor preaches sermons that are rooted in and filled with Scripture. At our church, my main points typically come out of one central Bible passage. Occasionally, when I'm delivering a topical message, I'll switch texts from point to point. But my goal is always to leave listeners impressed with God's Word, not with me as a communicator. A preacher's stories won't change your life long-term. Only God's Word will. So, listen with discernment.

Third, listen with a pen in hand. Communication experts tell us that we remember, at best, only 10 percent of what we hear. I hate that statistic, because I spend twenty to twenty-five hours a week preparing a sermon that people are going to *listen* to. And they're only going to remember 10 percent of it? How discouraging!

I know that I speak for all pastors when I say: Please, please, pretty please with sugar on top, pick up a pen and write down something as you're listening to a sermon. You'll get a better grip on God's Word by doing so. And you'll make your pastor's day! (Just a side note here: If you use a phone-app or e-reader for your Bible, don't let that keep you from writing something down. Either take notes on your phone/e-reader or use a pen and paper to record your insights.)

Fourth, listen with the aim of putting what you hear into practice. I was tuned in to a Christian radio station the other day—something I don't do a lot of—and a woman called in to express her gratitude for being able to listen to preachers all day long on that station. I immediately thought to myself: *How could she possibly put that much Bible teaching into practice?* She needs to turn her radio off! And if it sounds like I'm being too hard on her, James 1:22 puts it even more bluntly: "Do not merely listen to the word, and so deceive yourselves. Do what it says."

The ultimate aim of hearing God's Word is not Bible-*listening*; the ultimate aim is Bible-*doing*. That's one of the reasons that I gravitate toward teaching the Bible in topical series at my church. Now, from time to time someone will ask me why I don't do more "expository" teaching:

> **JAMES 1:22 puts it bluntly: "Do not merely listen to the word. . . . Do what it says."**

starting with the first verse of a book of the Bible and working my way through that book, verse after verse after verse. An occasional critic will even go so far as to suggest that a topical approach is for beginners, while a verse-by-verse approach is for mature believers.

Really? I usually ask that critic if Jesus was a topical preacher or a verse-by-verse guy. You see, Jesus could have gone through the Old Testament verse-by-verse, but that's not what you'll find in the Gospel accounts of His teaching, such as His famous Sermon on the Mount (Matthew 5–7). Jesus went from topic to topic.

The reason that I often teach God's Word topically (although we occasionally go through an entire book of the

Bible) is that it forces people to hear something again and again until they put it into practice. It may be four straight sermons on *prayer*, or three in a row on *wise money management*, or a five-part series on *parenting*—all rooted in Scripture. I intend to drive my listeners crazy until they *do* something with what they're hearing from God's Word. Make sense?

By the way, it's not my intention to disparage expository, verse-by-verse sermons. If that's your pastor's approach, great! I just want you to know that topical preaching can also be soundly biblical and have a major impact on listeners.

Get a Grip on Scripture by Reading

I'm a big fan of classical music. One of my favorite composers is Joseph Haydn, who wrote over a hundred symphonies during the eighteenth century. Recently I went to Amazon.com to purchase a good biography on Haydn. Their top recommendation was a book published back in 1904. Fortunately, I was able to track down a used copy of that book. And when it arrived in the mail, I was pumped.

You book lovers can appreciate this: I love the look, the feel, the smell of an old book. And I thought to myself: *People have been reading this very book for over a hundred years—since 1904.* Well . . . not exactly. As I began to read the book myself, I quickly discovered that about a third of the pages weren't even cut; they were still stuck together. I had to slice them apart in order to keep on reading. That means that while someone had *owned* this book for over a hundred years, nobody had actually *read* it!

If your Bible is still open to Nehemiah 8, circle the word "read" in verse 3: "[Ezra] read it [God's Word] aloud" to the people "from daybreak till noon." Now, go down to verse 8 and circle the same word: Ezra's buddies "read from the Book of the Law of God, making it clear."

Why did the people need Ezra and his coleaders to read the Bible aloud? Why didn't the people just read it for themselves? Well, besides the possibly that some of them were illiterate, they didn't have a personal copy of the Book of the Law. That's why they asked Ezra to break out *his* copy of the Scriptures and bring it to the town square (v. 1). He was the only guy who had a Bible (probably a leather-bound, gold-edged study Bible with a concordance and maps).

That's the same reason why the apostle Paul told a young pastor he was mentoring, Timothy, to devote himself to the public reading of Scripture (1 Timothy 4:13). The people in Timothy's church had no opportunity to read Scripture for themselves. But that's not true of us, is it? According to a recent poll, 95 percent of Christians say that they have a Bible in the house. In fact, those who identify themselves as "active" Christians have an average of six Bibles in the house! And 98 percent of those active Christians say that they actually *read* the Bible.[11]

That's the good news. But then the pollster asked a question that revealed some not-so-good news. How often do you read the Bible? Among those calling themselves active Christians, slightly more than one-third (35 percent) responded they read the Bible daily. Yet 19 percent read their Bible just two or three times a week. And 37 percent—almost four in ten active Christans—admit they read the Bible just one time a week or less.[12] Is it possible to be an "active" follower of Jesus Christ while ignoring His Word?

> ACCORDING TO one poll, among active Christians only 35 percent responded that they read the Bible daily.

If you're not yet a regular Bible reader, let me give you a few quick tips to get you started. Perhaps you've heard similar advice before. But as I noted earlier, I like to stay on a topic until people either *do* something about it or I drive them crazy!

First, *get yourself a solid study Bible.* There are several good ones available, but I personally like the *NIV* (New International Version) *Study Bible*, the work of a team of evangelical Hebrew and Greek scholars, and all the wonderful explanatory footnotes in the *NIV Study Bible*. Evidently, I'm not the only fan of the *NIV Study Bible*. There are more than seven million copies in print!

Second, *pick up a Bible reading schedule.* You'll find a read-through-the-Bible-in-four-years schedule online at *www.biblesavvy.com.* I prefer this pace over one-year reading plans, which *may* give you a complete read-through in twelve months, but often will leave you falling behind and unable to finish in one year. More on the advantages of the four-year plan appear in *Walk* (book four of the Bible Savvy series), where we delve into the topic of Bible application.

Third, *choose a time and a place for daily Bible reading.* If you're like me, it may be best to do your reading first thing in the morning. Otherwise, once the day gets going it's almost impossible to stop everything and carve out a niche of time for Bible reading. Where's the best place to do it? I have a friend who arrives at work early and sits in his truck in the parking lot to read his Bible. Other friends do it on the treadmill, or

READ WHEN you don't feel like it and when other distractions are pulling you to put your Bible down.

at a corner table at Starbucks, or in their favorite chair in the family room—wherever there's a little bit of privacy and a good chance of developing a habit.

Fourth, *just do it!* Read when you don't feel like it. Read when the reading schedule's chapter for the day is in the book of Ezekiel and you have a hard time figuring out how to apply it to your life. Read when other distractions are pulling you to put your Bible down and pay attention to them. A lot of people find it helpful to make it a rule not to engage in any other leisure activity until they've read God's Word for the day. No newspaper reading, no Facebooking, no eating breakfast, no working out, no texting a friend—nothing before the Bible.

Not too long ago, I received an email from someone who has been attending our church for a few years. He wrote about how both his relationship with God and his marriage have begun to blossom. And then he explained how all that got started. He'd heard me challenge everybody to buy an *NIV Study Bible*, pick up a reading schedule, and get after it. So he did. This is what he wrote in his email to me:

"I changed my schedule in the mornings, started waking up 30 minutes earlier and would take that time to read from the Bible. Since then I've done pretty well at reading at least 5 times a week. Sure, I slipped here and there . . . but each time I rededicated myself."

Now, read the close of his email: "This morning I finished the Bible, cover to cover. This was very important to me, because I stopped messing around and really started to dig into Christianity and the Word of God. I began to become much more engaged with the sermons, because I had either already read the Bible texts or would be reading them soon. . . . God willing, I will continue reading and learning from His Word my whole life. By my calculations, I should be able to read through the whole thing another 25 times minimum. It's made a real difference in my life."

This guy not only encouraged his pastor but also laid down a solid foundation for himself by reading through the entire Bible.

Get a Grip on Scripture by Studying

Let's go back to Nehemiah 8 and look again at the closing verse of our passage (v. 8). God's people were not merely hearing the Bible and reading the Bible. They were digging into it. Their leaders were explaining the Bible's meaning to them, helping them to understand the text and apply it to their lives.

I've got good news for you. You can do this for yourself these days. I'm not suggesting that you don't need the regular input of a Bible-teaching pastor. I've already covered the importance of that. I'm just challenging you to do your own study as well, with the assistance of a good study Bible that will explain difficult passages and with the camaraderie of a small group. (I hope your church offers small groups that meet to discuss and apply Scripture.)

Studying the Bible is not an option for genuine Christ followers. God expects us to become expert handlers of His Word.

That requires going beyond merely reading the text. It

entails drilling down into specific verses, looking up the cross-references that your study Bible supplies, and recording your insights and applications in a journal or filling in the study guide that your small group is using.

As the apostle Paul puts it, "Do your best to present yourself to God as one approved, a workman who does not need to be ashamed and who correctly handles the word of truth" (2 Timothy 2:15). Are you becoming skilled at handling God's Word? It doesn't happen overnight. It doesn't happen without effort. It doesn't happen without studying.

We may be tempted to object, "I don't have that kind of time." Or, "I never was very good in school." Or, "This sounds like Christianity 501, but I'm content with 101 or 201." But shouldn't we be so hungry for God's Word that we push past excuses like these?

Allow me to embarrass all of us for just a moment by comparing our sometimes meager appetite for the Bible with the ravenous hunger for it in other parts of the world. Here are a couple of quick snapshots I want you to look at. The first snapshot is from my most recent *Voice of the Martyrs* news magazine. (*VOM* is an organization that supports persecuted Christ followers around the world.) It's a picture of Ahmed, a truck driver in Egypt. Ahmed has been repeatedly arrested and tortured by the Egyptian secret police. Why? Because Ahmed is a Christ follower.

But worse than that, Ahmed has supplied Bibles to a group of forty-two former Muslims who have become Christ followers. And these men were not just Muslims—they were members of a radical group called the Muslim Brotherhood. Ahmed has refused to tell the Egyptian secret police where these guys are hiding—even though they hung him upside down and beat him.[13]

But Ahmed did tell *VOM* that the last time he'd visited his new Christian friends they'd just finished going through the Bible for the eighth time. The eighth time! How many of us have been through it once?

The second snapshot is a group picture described in Charles Colson's book *The Faith*. It's a pretty big group. It's the church in China. Back in 1949, Mao Tse-tung began to systematically persecute these believers. Anyone caught in possession of a Bible was tortured or thrown into prison. Or just plain executed.

In spite of that threat, Christ followers have been hand copying the Bible so that they can read and study it on their own. And if an underground church is fortunate enough to have its own copy of the Bible, it's usually broken up into a number of portions and distributed among the church's members. That way, if any of their houses are raided by the secret police and one portion of the Bible is confiscated, they won't lose the whole thing.

Christ followers have even dug up the graves of believers who died before Mao came to power, because there is often a Bible in the coffin. Anything to get a Bible that can be read and studied. When Mao began to persecute the church in 1949, there were four million Christ followers in China. Now, there are an estimated 80 million or more.[14]

After looking at snapshots like these, any excuses we offer for not studying the Bible on our own and in small groups sound pretty lame.

Get a Grip on Scripture by Memorizing and Meditating

My older sister, Kathy, has a master's degree in piano performance. When I was growing up, I was subjected to hearing her practice four to five hours every day. During her high school years, she won several prestigious piano competitions. I can still hum the melodies of the pieces that she played in those contests because she rehearsed them again and again and again.

Interestingly, the very first thing that Kathy would do when she was learning a piece was to memorize it. That's a twist, isn't it? Most of us who grew up taking piano lessons only memorized pieces after we'd worked on them for weeks and weeks. But if you're a pro, you memorize the piece first and *then* you start working on it. You don't set the tempos, add the dynamics, or shape the phrases until you know the piece by heart.

This is very similar to how we should approach memorizing and meditating on God's Word. If we would first *memorize* a Bible verse or two, we could then go to work on that text. We could *meditate* on it, which simply means to turn it over and over in our minds, squeezing insights out of it, reflecting on what it teaches us about God, and considering ways it might be applied in our lives.

So memorizing and meditating go together. First we memorize, then we meditate on what's been memorized. Interestingly, the Bible doesn't even bother to use the word *memorize.* Not because memorizing God's Word is unimportant but because meditating (a word the Bible *does* use frequently) presupposes memorizing.

Of course, another reason the Bible doesn't bother to use the word *memorize* is because there are many colorful expressions that it employs in place of that word. Moses tells us, for example, to bind God's Word on our foreheads (Deuteronomy 6:8). The psalmist encourages us to hide God's Word in our hearts (Psalm 119:11). The prophet Ezekiel says that he ate God's Word and it was sweet to his taste (Ezekiel 3:3). Jesus asks us to allow His words to remain in us, like branches remain in a vine (John 15:7). The apostle Paul writes: "Let the word of Christ dwell in you"; that is, let it set up residency in your life (Colossians 3:16). All of these pictures suggest that we should be memorizing Scripture, even if the word *memorize* is never used.

But memorizing verses from the Bible still sounds like a daunting task, doesn't it? Some of us complain that we have lousy memories. But that isn't true. We've memorized all sorts of things: our social security number; the words to the "Star Spangled Banner"; the birthdays of family members; our bike lock combination; the name of our kindergarten teacher. (My teacher's name was Mrs. Polkinghorn. How cool a name is that for a kindergarten teacher?)

There's nothing wrong with our memories. And there's nothing more important to memorize than God's Word. Let me tell you three benefits that you'll experience when you memorize portions of the Bible. These three benefits are mentioned in the opening three verses of Psalm 1:

> Blessed is the man who does not walk in the counsel
> of the wicked or stand in the way of sinners
> or sit in the seat of mockers.
> But his delight is in the law of the Lord,
> and on his law he meditates day and night.
> He is like a tree planted by streams of water,
> which yields its fruit in season and whose leaf
> does not wither.
> Whatever he does prospers.

The first benefit of memorizing is *the Bible will become portable*. In the middle of this passage, the psalmist describes a person who is able to meditate on God's Word *day and night*. Let me point out the obvious. In order to meditate on God's Word *day and night*, you either have to have a copy of the Bible constantly open in front of you (along with a flashlight if it's the middle of the night), or you have to know portions of the Bible by memory, right?

When you know portions of the Bible by memory, you can take the Bible with you wherever you go. You can pull out a key verse when you're offering counsel to a friend, or when you're praising God on a starry night, or when you're wrestling with a difficult decision, or when you're passing time while washing the dishes. The Bible will become portable.

The second benefit of memorizing is *the Bible will become preventive*. Look again at the opening verse of Psalm 1. The psalmist warns us not to get sucked into temptation. We've got to resist: the counsel of the wicked, the way of sinners, and the seat of mockers. How do we do that? The answer is in verse 2: by *meditating* on the Bible (i.e., those verses that we've memorized).

WHEN WE memorize Scripture, the Bible becomes portable, preventive, and productive in our lives.

Psalm 119:11 puts it this way: "I have hidden your word

in my heart that I might not sin against you." When we know verses from the Bible by memory, the Holy Spirit has something to bring to our minds when we're facing temptation. This is how Jesus defended Himself when Satan tempted Him in the wilderness. Satan threw three different temptations at Jesus (Matthew 4) and Jesus fought back with three different Scripture verses, each of them from the book of Deuteronomy. Deuteronomy! When was the last time we even *read* Deuteronomy, much less *memorized* portions of it?

The apostle Paul warns us that the Devil and his evil cohorts are constantly scheming against us. How are we to protect ourselves against their attacks? Paul tells us that God has given us six pieces of spiritual armor that must be put on every day. (See Ephesians 6:10-17.) The last piece of armor on the list is "the sword of the Spirit, which is the word of God." Perhaps if we would memorize some *preventive* Bible verses, we would lose fewer battles with Satan.

SATAN THREW three different temptations at Jesus, who fought back with three different Scripture verses.

The final benefit of memorizing is *the Bible will become productive.* The last verse in the Psalm 1 passage paints a great picture of a person who memorizes and meditates on God's Word: he or she is a fruitful tree, never withering, always prospering. Does that describe your life? It could, if you are willing to invest some time in memorizing Scripture, which could then be brought to mind throughout the day.

How to Memorize Scripture

Let me get real practical. Sometimes we just need a few simple how-tos to get us started down the path of a new behavior. Here are four basic tips that will help you develop the habit of memorizing the Bible.

Tip 1: Record a text. Pick out a Bible verse (or verses) that you'd like to memorize and write it down on a 3 x 5 card. It might be a verse about God that moves you, or speaks of some character virtue that you'd like to develop, or that sums up what you recently learned in a sermon or small group lesson—whatever. You might even decide to start with an entire chapter of the Bible, like Psalm 1. (It's only six verses long.) Write out the verses of that chapter on some 3 x 5 cards.

Joe White is a former college football coach, the director of a premier youth sports camp, and a parenting expert. Dr. White raised four outstanding boys of his own. And before they were given the car keys for the first time as teenagers, they had to recite the entire New Testament book of Philippians! (That's four chapters; 104 verses.) Joe says that Bible memorization was the greatest shaping influence in his sons' lives.[15]

When people ask Joe where to begin memorizing the Bible, he always responds: "With verse 1." "Verse 1 of what?" people want to know. "Verse 1 of your favorite chapter" is Joe's reply. "But then what?" they ask. "Well, then you go on to verse 2." So what are you waiting for? Record a text.

Tip 2: Repeat one line at a time. You've heard the expression "rote memory"? The word *rote* suggests the use of routine or repetition. There's really no trick to memorizing a Bible verse other than to repeat the first line of it again and again and again, until you can say it without looking at it. And then you move on to the second line. It's a good idea to start your memorizing with the reference. That way you'll remember where to find the verse in the Bible, even if you forget the verse itself.

Tip 3: Recruit a partner. Every week hundreds of grade school children attend our church's Awana program. In addition to participating in lots of fun and games, these kids are learning scores of Bible verses by heart. This necessitates that moms and dads listen to their recitations during the week. So, from time to time I challenge the parents in our congregation to occasionally turn the tables at home and ask their children to listen to the Bible verses that mom and dad are memorizing. Of course, that assumes that mom and dad *are* memorizing Bible verses. What a great example to set for the kids!

Sue and I are almost always working on some Bible

memory project together. John 15, Isaiah 40, Romans 8, and various psalms are some of the favorite passages that we've committed to memory. It's wonderful, on a long car ride or walk along the river, to review these portions of God's Word with each other.

At this writing my mom is eighty-five years old and still memorizing the Bible! Last January she called from Florida, where my parents winter, to tell me that she was working on Romans 8 (all thirty-nine verses) and hoped to quote it to me when she returned home in April. Then she threw down the gauntlet, challenging me to be able to recite it with her at that time.

Tip 4: Recite word-perfect. When you're reviewing your verses with your partner, ask to be corrected if you don't recite the verses word-perfect. This isn't because you want to be a perfectionist. It's because it's easier to memorize something if you repeat it the same way every time.

Well, that concludes my tips for memorizing the Bible. I hope you'll put into practice what you learned in this chapter. My prayer is that you'll *Get a Grip* on God's Word by hearing, reading, studying, memorizing, and meditating. At the risk of mixing my metaphors, let me add that it takes getting a grip on God's Word in order for it to become a rock-solid *foundation* for your life.

Study Guide

Icebreaker

What media-related activity is most likely to keep you from reading good books?

1. Read Nehemiah 8:1–8 and note anything that strikes you about the way in which these people listened to God's Word.

2. Which of the four Bible-hearing tips would be most helpful if you put it into practice? Why?

3. How many Bibles are there in your home (guess-timate)? How many days a week (be honest) do you sit down and read the Bible? If you read it less than three times a week, what keeps you from being a more consistent reader? If you

read it three or more times a week, what has helped this become your regular habit?

(icon) What is (or would be) the best time of the day and location for you to read the Bible? Why?

4. How does *studying* the Bible differ from merely *reading* it?

5. (icon) What are the benefits of studying the Bible with a group of people?

6. What is the relationship between *memorizing* and *meditating on* the Bible?

What are some good reasons for you to memorize portions of the Bible? (If you have already become a Bible-memorizer, feel free to add your own reasons to the three that are mentioned in *Foundation*.)

7. Choose a text to memorize and write it out on a 3 x 5 card. What passage did you choose, and why?

8. (speech bubble icon) Do a quick review of *Foundation* and write out your best takeaway from each of the four chapters.

"God's Autobiography"

"Lost in Transmission?"

"The Only Way to Know"

"Get a Grip"

Notes

About the Bible Savvy Series

1. Thom S. Rainer, *The Unchurched Next Door* (Grand Rapids: Zondervan, 2003), 200.

Introduction: A Rock-Solid Foundation

1. "Plane Crash Devastates Marshall University," This Day in History, http://www.history.com/this-day-in-history/plane-crash-devastates-marshall-university.

2. George Keith, "How Firm a Foundation," *Inspiring Hymns* (Grand Rapids: Zondervan, 1968), in public domain.

Chapter 1: God's Autobiography (Doctrine of Inspiration)

1. Libby Hill, "How Did an 1885 Flood of Little Consequence Become an Epidemic that 'Killed' 90,000 Chicagoans?" *Chicago Tribune*, 29 July 2007, 16 ff.; see also http://faculty.ccc.edu/jtassin/geology201/homework/Chicagogeo/cholera.htm.

2. Ibid. The *Chicago Tribune* corrected the story in 2005 and published Hill's article "How Did an 1885 Flood of Little Consequence Become an Epidemic?" in 2007, but later in 2007 it reverted to the erroneous statistic that one of every eight Chicagoans died in the alleged epidemic. See "Corrections and Clarifications," *Chicago Tribune*, 29 September 2005, http://articles.chicagotribune.com/2005-09-29/news/0509290134_1_section-epidemic-incorrect-first; and "Chicago's Legendary Epidemic," *Chicago Tribune*, 22 August 2007, http://articles.chicagotribune.com/2007-08-22/news/0708210481_1_cholera-epidemic-chicago-river-metropolitan-water-reclamation-district.

3. Hill, "How Did an 1885 Flood of Little Consequence Become an Epidemic?"

4. Ibid. See also Libby Hill, *The Chicago River: A Natural and Unnatural History* (Chicago: Lake Claremont Press, 2000), 116–17.

5. Ibid.

6. John Kandell, "The Glorious History of Handel's Messiah, *Smithsonian*, December 2009, http://www.smithso nianmag.com/arts-culture/The-Glorious-History-of-Handels-Messiah.html#ixzz28FotSiRc; also "Handel's 'Messiah' Inspires Listeners, Transcends Time," CBN News, broadcast 16 December 2011, http://www.cbn.com/cbn-news/us/2011/December/Handels-Messiah-Inspires-Listen-ers-Transcends-Time/.

7. Lee Strobel, *The Case for Christ* (Grand Rapids: Zondervan, 1998), 98.

8. For example, both Matthew and Luke tell the story of Satan tempting Jesus in the desert. Both describe the same three enticements, but they differ on the order in which the temptations were presented. A closer inspection of the two texts reveals that Matthew is following a chronological order (indicated by his use of words like "then" and "again"), while Luke is tying the temptations together without any reference to a time continuum. So Matthew tells us that Satan's second temptation was to entice Jesus to hurl Himself from the pinnacle of the temple, but Luke treats this as the third and final temptation—perhaps because it's the most climactic of the three (cf. Matthew 4:1–11; Luke 4:1–13).

Chapter 2: *Lost in Transmission?* (History of the Canon)

1. Nathan Ausubel, "Sofer," *The Book of Jewish Knowledge* (New York: Crown, 1964), 420. An *iota* is the nearest Greek equivalent to the Hebrew *yodh*, the smallest letter of the Hebrew alphabet.

2. Bart Ehrman, *Misquoting Jesus: The Story Behind Who Changed the Bible and Why* (New York: HarperOne, 2007).

3. Lee Strobel, *The Case for the Real Jesus* (Grand Rapids: Zondervan, 2007), 69–99.

4. Dan Brown, *The Da Vinci Code* (New York: Anchor, 2009).

5. Liz Halloran, "Lloyd Bentsen to Dan Quayle: 'Senator, You Are No Jack Kennedy,'" *US News*, 17 January 2008, http://www.usnews.com/news/articles/2008/01/17/the-mother-of-all-put-downs.

6. Grant Osborne, "Decoding the DaVinci Code," *Trinity Magazine*, Fall 2004, 20.

7. Rebecca Leung, "New Questions on Bush Guard Duty," *CBS News*, 11 February 2009; the transcript of the 8 September 2004 broadcast on *60 Minutes* can be found at http://www.cbsnews.com//2100-500164_162-641984.html.

8. Ibid.

9. Maureen Balleza and Kate Zernike, "Memos on Bush Are Fake but Accurate, Typist Says," *New York Times*, 15 September 2004; http://www.nytimes.com/2004/09/15/politics/campaign/15guard.html.

10. As quoted in Lee Strobel, *The Case for Christ* (Grand Rapids: Zondervan, 1998), 97.

11. William M. Ramsay, *The Bearing of Recent Discovery on the Trustworthiness of the New Testament* (Grand Rapids: Baker, 1953), http://www.blueletterbible.org/faq/don_stewart/stewart.cfm?id=804; http://www.bibleevidences.com/archeology.htm.

12. Gospel of Thomas 7:1–2, as cited in Ron Cameron, *The Other Gospels: Non-Canonical Gospel Texts* (Westminster Press, 1982), 26.

13. Gospel of Thomas 22:4–7, quoted in ibid., 28.

Chapter 3: The Only Way to Know (Doctrine of Revelation)

1. C. S. Lewis, *Reflections on the Psalms* (New York: Harcourt, Brace, World, 1958), 63.

2. Nicholas Perrin, *Lost in Transmission?* (Nashville: Nelson, 2009).

3. See http://www.Navigators.org/resources/shared/tools/bridge.pdf for a copy of the Navigators' illustration of the bridge, complete with tips, text, and Bible verses for using the bridge as an evangelistic tool.

Chapter 4: Get a Grip (Means of Learning)

1. Chart, "Percentage of Adults in Each Prose, Document, and Quantitative Literacy Level: 1992 and 2003," in National Assessment of Adult Literacy, 2003, http://nces.ed.gov/naal/kf_demographics.asp. The survey, published by the Institute of Education Sciences, shows 43 percent of adults read prose at "basic" or "below basic" levels.

2. "To Read or Not to Read," Research Report #47, National Endowment for the Arts, Washington, D.C., November 2007, 7.

3. Ibid., 9.

4. Amanda Lenhart et al., "Teens, Social Networking, Mobile, Generations, Blogs, Web 2.0: Social Media and Young Adults," Pew Internet and American Life Project, 3 February 2010, http://pewinternet.org/Reports/2010/Social-Media-and-Young-Adults.aspx.

5. "100 Million iPods Sold," Apple Inc., 9 April 2007.

6. "The Twitter Revolution," *The Week*, 23 April 2009, at http://theweek.com/article/index/95694/the-twitter-revolution.

7. "Review: *The Shallows: What the Internet Is Doing to Our Brains*," *The Week*, 18 June 2010, 24.

8. During midyear 2009, according to a report by Facebook's Inside Facebook: Justin Smith, "Facebook Now Growing by over 700,000 Users a Day, and New Engagement Stats," 2 July 2009, at http://www.insidefacbook.com/2009/07/02/facebook-now-growing-by-over-700000-users-a-day-updated-engagement-stats/.

9. Barbara Ortutay, "Facebook Now Home to 1 Billion Monthly Users," *Businessweek*, 4 October 2012, at http://www.businessweek.com/ap/2012-10-04/facebook-tops-1-billion-users.

10. For more information on what the Navigators calls "The Word Hand," see http://www.navigators.org/us/resources/illustrations/items/The%20Word%20Hand.

11. Sam O'Neal, "American Christians and Bible Reading," *Christianity Today*, Spring 2009, R7.

12. Ibid., R9.

13. Tom White, "Loving the Ugliest," *VOM Magazine*, January 2011.

14. Charles Colson, *The Faith* (Grand Rapids: Zondervan, 2008), 44.

15. Joe White, *Faith Training* (Carol Stream, Ill.: Tyndale, 1994), 54.

Bibliography

Geisler, Norman and Thomas Howe. *When Critics Ask: A Popular Handbook on Bible Difficulties*. Wheaton: Victor Books, 1992.

Keller, Timothy. *The Reason for God*. New York: Riverhead Trade, 2009.

Perrin, Nicholas. *Lost in Transmission?* Nashville: Nelson, 2009.

Strobel, Lee. *The Case for Christ*. Grand Rapids: Zondervan, 1998.

———. *The Case for the Real Jesus*. Grand Rapids: Zondervan, 2007.

Wright, Christopher. *The God I Don't Understand*. Grand Rapids: Zondervan, 2008.

JAMES L. NICODEM

Bible Savvy

Epic: The Storyline of the Bible unveils the single theme that ties all of scripture together: redemption.

Foundation: The Trustworthiness of the Bible explains where our current bible came from and why it can be wholly trusted.

Context: How to Understand the Bible shows readers how to read the different parts of the Bible as they were meant to be read and how they fit together.

Walk: How to Apply the Bible puts the readers increased understanding of the Bible into real life terms and contexts.